FROM

HOT MESS

TO

HALLELUJAH

THE TRANSFORMATION POWER OF "I AM"

by Stephanie Anderson

FORWARD

It's astonishing to read about your own death on social media months after it was posted, but that's how I found out about it. Even when I saw the red tag on my wrist that said "Bank – Blood Bank", it didn't register with me. Strangely enough, no one had ever mentioned it to me at that time, so I didn't know. Even stranger, why me? I was a homeless, drug addicted prostitute with a bad attitude. Why would God choose me? My own family had given up on me. I had given up on myself. I tried many times to end my life because I thought that my family would be better off without me. Even then, God wouldn't let me die. On January 16, 2020, in the quiet obscurity of a Neurological ICU room, I drew my last breath. I had been taken off life support. There were no doctors or nurses with me, no one there to try to revive me. It was entirely the power of God that brought me back to life, filling my body with new life, my lungs with the very breath of God Himself. Three days later I woke up with a calling on my life- to spend the rest of my life helping other people who are just like I was, helping them to feel less broken and lead them to the God who saved me.

"Jesus said to her, "I am the resurrection and the life. He who believes in Me, though he may die, he shall live. And whoever lives and believes in Me shall never die. Do you believe this?'

John 11:25-26

If you would like to contact the author, or if you would like to give a donation to make "From HOT MESS To HALLELUJAH" available free of charge to inmates and women in shelters and transitional recovery centers, please email:

<u>hotmess2hallelujah@gmail.com</u>

Or send donations directly to Cash App at $hotmess2hallelujah

You may also write to:

Stephanie Anderson

1300 Joseph E. Boone Blvd.

Atlanta, GA 30314

It has been my prayer since the first word of this book for God to transform lives, to lead people to Jesus, and to use those people to bring others into God's Kingdom. If this book has helped you, I would love to hear about it, although the only thing that really matters is that you are living the life God called you to live, a life of freedom, purpose, and love. I still pray for the readers of this book every day, because I know prayer is powerful and God hears every prayer. Many blessings to you.

Stephanie

100% of all donations are used for the purpose of sending this book to women in jails, prisons, homeless shelters, and transitional recovery centers. Thank you for helping make that possible.

JUST SO YOU KNOW...

This book was written to let you know that you've been lied to your whole life. You may have even believed the lies, like I did. I'm no expert. I don't have a theology degree. I didn't go to seminary. I didn't even finish high school. But I am living proof, tangible evidence, of the transforming power of who God says I am. My prayer is that you will know that you know that you know, without a shadow of a doubt, that God can give you an amazing, beautiful, brand new life, not just in the sweet by and by, but in the right here right now.

There's a lot of my life in this book. Not because I want to be the center of attention, but because I want you to see for yourself, to know, that if God can turn my life around, He can surely do that for you, too. I know that I'm not the only one that's ever felt hopeless, helpless, trapped, ashamed, angry, defeated, depressed, unwanted, unloved, cast out, hurt, rejected, abused, worthless, forgotten, and used. I know that I can't be the only one that was just waiting for life to be done with. I can't be the only one that just tried to make it through each day as numb as possible, from one drug to the next, secretly hoping that somehow they would put a permanent end to the pain of surviving any given day. There's no way that I am the only person that fought against demons both in the people around me and in my own mind. I know I'm not the only one. This book is especially for those people.

For everything I've ever been through in my life, I am grateful, because by living the life that I've lived, I am able to connect with anybody, to look a person in the eye and honestly say, "I understand. I know what you're going through, because I've been there, too, but listen to what God did for me. He will do the same for you." That's an enormous blessing, to go from being less than nothing to a soldier for Christ! I'm still a hot mess, but now I'm holy and blessed. And so are you. You'll see.

DO NOT BE DECIEVED, GOD IS NOT MOCKED

"Take a good look, friends, at who you were when you got called into this life. I don't see many of "the brightest and the best" among you, not many influential, not many from high-society families. Isn't it obvious that God deliberately chose men and women that the culture overlooks and exploits and abuses, chose these "nobodies" to expose the hollow pretensions of the "somebodies"?" – 1 Corinthians 1:26-28, The Message Translation

The prison system in Georgia was so backed up, people were paroling straight out of county jails. Five counties sued the state to allow inmates into the prisons. I was on the 2nd run out, having spent 14 months waiting to go to Metro State Prison in Atlanta. It was nowhere close to my first time being locked up. I was comfortable there. Most of the people I was locked up with were people I knew from the streets. I knew most of the guards from having been locked up so many times. My days were passed sleeping, (which I rarely did on the outside), drawing or painting with paint I made from the coating off candy, playing cards for commissary, reading, or stirring up trouble. The cell I was in was a large, open population cell with 60-plus other women. I didn't like any of them. There was a small population of women, maybe 12 or so, that held a Bible study every day. They took up the only 2 long, steel tables we had in the dorm. I don't know why, but I decided to interrupt them one day. At first, I just taunted them, telling them that if they had been doing all that Bible study out in the streets, they wouldn't be locked up. They never even responded. I took that to mean that I was right, and their "jailhouse religion" wasn't fooling anybody. Every day I would stop by their tables with the same old thing, but I turned up the heat. "If y'all had put down your crackpipes and picked up your Bibles out there, you wouldn't be sitting in here." They never took the bait, so I came up with a few questions for them. "How do you know God is real? You can't touch Him. You can't see Him. If God is real, how come He doesn't get you out of here? I want to know He's real like this wall." And I would slap the painted cinderblock wall behind me. "I can see the wall. I can touch the wall. Y'all can't even prove He's real! All y'all trying to do is get out early. Ain't nobody going to let you out till you do your time, so you might as well wrap it up." No one ever said a single word to me. I couldn't say anything to provoke or offend even one woman at those 2 tables, much less pick a fight, no matter how hard I tried.

NEW LIFE FROM THE WORD OF GOD

"During the fourth watch of the night (In your darkest hour,) Jesus went out to them (Jesus is with you, even in this jail.), walking on the lake (Jesus is over the storm. He's on top of every storm that will

ever come against you.). When the disciples saw Him walking on the lake, they were terrified. "It's a ghost," (The Spirit of Christ is alive!) they said, and cried out in fear. (Cry out to God!) But Jesus immediately said to them: (Immediately Jesus will answer you) "Take courage! It is I. Don't be afraid." (I am real. I am with you. I will save you.) "Lord, if it's You," Peter replied, "tell me to come to You on the water." (Jesus, I need You! How do I get there?) "Come," He said. (Jesus is calling you to come to Him.)Then Peter got down out of the boat, (Step out in faith.) walked on the water and came toward Jesus. (Nothing is impossible for Me.) But when he saw the wind, (Don't take your eyes off Jesus and don't look at the circumstances around you.), he was afraid (Don't be afraid. I am with you. Trust Me.) and, beginning to sink, (If you take Your eyes off Me, you're on your own.) cried out, " Lord, save me!"(It's never too late to cry out "Save me, Jesus!")" – Matthew 14:25-30, NIV, (Words in parentheses added.)

Sleeping all day and staying up all night made my days go by faster, or so it seemed. Nighttime was the only time I could have total peace and quiet. The roar of inmates around me during the day served as a droning lullaby, much like the *whoosh* sound vehicles would make years later when I lived under a bridge over the highway. Head count was at 5 am. A handful of women would stay awake, waiting on breakfast or the morning newspaper. A few weeks after I started harassing the women's Bible study, I was the only person that stayed up after head count. That didn't even cross my mind until later, but it was a set up from God Himself. I was just glad for the quiet time. Both the newspaper and breakfast were late and I was bored. We didn't have a television, but I saw a book lying open on another table. I went to see if it was one I hadn't read. It was a Bible, and it was turned to Matthew 14. I never read the Bible, because I couldn't understand it or remember what I had read. The few things I was able to grasp didn't make sense to me, and since I knew everything back then, if I didn't get it, there must have been something wrong with it. My eyes went straight to Matthew 14:25, and as I was reading, there was a voice, not one I could hear with my ears, or even so much a thought that I heard in my head. The voice was from somewhere *inside of me,* coming from someplace like my upper belly, but with a soft grab to it. The words in parentheses that are added to the Scripture above are those words. When I saw the lady that seemed to be the one that led the Bible studies, BangBang, I blocked her path. No "Good morning". No breakfast, even. I demanded an answer to a question I didn't even know how to ask. I wanted to know what had happened. I did my best to try to explain, but nothing I said made sense. She told me that I had had a revelation. I became angry and told her, "No, I told you it was in *Matthew*! Not Revelation!" She obviously wasn't even listening to me. She laughed at me. I started cussing her out. She cut me off, though, and told me that she wasn't laughing *at me*, and explained that revelation was when God reveals something to you by His Spirit that you couldn't know any other way. I still couldn't wrap my mind around it. And I was drained, physically exhausted. I had been in the Spirit for about 2 hours, and the experience of being born again put me into a solid sleep for 2 days. I must have gotten up for 5 am and 5 pm head count, but I honestly have no recollection of it.

I AM THAT I AM

BangBang ordered a Recovery Bible from the chaplain for me. I told her that I had tried to read the Bible many times, but it didn't make sense to me. She told me to start with the stuff written in the boxes, the commentary. I did that. As I read, if it talked about Scriptures, I would jump over and read a verse or two. Before long, I found myself reading *and understanding* what I had read. Then I started devouring the Word, and the Word took me outside of the jail. Even though I was still physically locked up, I felt free for the first time in my life. I had real joy, real peace. I knew that if I spent the rest of my life in a cell, nothing could take away what had been given to me through God's Word. Even now, I can't find the right words to explain it, but I knew it was more real than anything else that I could see, hear, or touch. There was another woman locked up with us named Angel that was always getting in trouble, even in jail. She had a lot of anger. Like me, she had been arrested over and over again and didn't have anyone that visited her, but one day a woman came to visit her that definitely wasn't "one of us". Although I didn't see her the first time she came, when I did see her, I noticed she was pretty and dressed really nice, but not like she was trying to dress up. She always smiled and it was a real smile, the kind where you could see the smile in her eyes, too. How Angel, who was no angel at all, could possibly be in the same family as this other lady mystified me. One day Angel came back from a visit with some papers and I overheard her talking about what they were. The lady wasn't her family. She was from a church. She had given her a list that said "Angel is (something from the Bible)" with the location of where it was in the Bible typed next to it. Wow! I had never imagined such a thing. I asked her if I could look at it. There were 2 pages, with line after line of "Angel is ...." and the Scripture reference next to each one. I wanted one of those, too! I wanted it so bad, but I had no idea where to get it, or even how to ask for it, since I really didn't even know what it was, much less who to ask. I never forgot about that list, though. The thought of it stayed with me until I got out of prison. Since I had never heard of "identity in Christ", I used my cousin's computer and started looking up "I am" on the internet. I printed out some of the things that I found and made my own list. That's where I came across the term "identity in Christ". I was able to get a better understanding of what it meant, and the more I studied it, the more God revealed to me about it and what to do with it. I started speaking those words every morning. My list got longer as I began to look on my own who God said I was in His Word. I found myself getting up 2 hours early every day to spend time in prayer, worship, and speaking God's Word out loud. On the few occasions

15

when I overslept, I found that if I didn't get that time with the Lord, my day was seriously off-track. On the days that I gave God first priority, though, I began to see myself through God's eyes. For the first time in my life, I had hope, I was confident, I had great self esteem, and I even felt beautiful and brand new. God showed me divine favor. I applied for a job that paid well, but I had to take a drug test and pass a background check. For the first time in my life, I passed a drug test, but it was God that took over the background check. I had just gotten out of prison and had a long criminal record, yet my background came back clear. I got the job, which paid well, but having a little money in my pocket, I did what I knew to do with it. I got high. I backslid for 20 years, but when I came back, God was just like the prodigal son's father. (Luke 15:11-32) He saw me from afar off and met me where I was. He welcomed me back with open arms. Again, the "I am …." started whispering to me.

"AS I LIVE", SAYS THE LORD, "JUST AS YOU HAVE SPOKEN IN MY HEARING, SO I WILL DO TO YOU".

"Death and life are in the power of the tongue and those who love it will eat its fruit."

Proverbs 18:21

Our words have power, whether good or bad. God spoke all of creation into existence. (Gen. 1:3-26, Ps. 33:9) No matter what you may be going through or what your life may look like right now, God's Word is your answer. God's Word is Truth. (Jn. 17:17) God's Word is Spirit and Life. (Jn. 6:63) God's Word is living and powerful. (Heb. 4:12) Since God's Word is Truth, anything that does not agree with it is a lie. (Jn. 8:32, 36) The lies we believe, from other people, society, the media, even our own thoughts, are ultimately from the devil, the father of all lies. (Jn. 8:44, Jn. 10:10)

When we speak God's Word out loud, (not just in our minds,) we are bringing it into being. (Mk. 11:23) God watches over His Word to perform it. (Jer. 1:12) When we speak God's Word out loud, believing in the God who promised it, we will get our healing, our peace, our purpose, and our blessings. God's Word cannot come back to Him without accomplishing the thing that it was sent out to do. (Is. 55:11)

"I don't think the way you think. The way you work isn't the way I work. God's Decree. For as the skies soar high above the earth, so the way I work surpasses the way you work, and the way I think is beyond the way you think. Just as rain and snow descend from the skies and don't go back until they've watered the earth, doing their work of making things grow and blossom, producing seed for farmers and food for the hungry, so will the words that come out of My mouth not come back empty handed. They'll do the work I sent

17

them to do, they'll complete the assignment I gave them. So you'll go out in joy, you'll be led into a whole and complete life."

Isaiah 55:8-12,

The Message Bible

When God hears us speak His Word, He sends His angels forth to make it happen. (Ps. 103:20) "Heeding the voice of His Word" means doing what God's Word says. The Word is God's, but the voice is ours. We are the voice of God's Word. (Job 22:28, Jer. 23:28) Jesus said in Luke 10:16:"He who hears you hears Me..."

Speaking God's Word has to be done in faith. (2 Cor. 5:7, Rom. 10:8) Faith simply means "believing" (2 Cor. 4:13) or "trusting". (Prov. 3:5, Rom. 10:17) The more you get to know God, the more you will trust Him. He will never, ever let you down, lie to you, or leave you. He is faithful. (Heb. 10:23) Speaking God's Word gives us faith and faith gives us hope. (Heb. 11:1) Hope gives us endurance, the ability to hang in there when things get tough. (1 Thes. 1:3) Jesus said in Mark 9:23: "If you can believe, all things are possible to him who believes."And in Luke 1:37, "For with God nothing will be impossible."

We become what we believe. (Prov. 23:7) We believe what we speak. Regardless of how things look, feel, sound, what people say, what you read, what you hear, or even what you think yourself, faith

18

believes the truth of what God says. (Rom. 4:17) Whatever the Bible says you are, you have, you can do, that is the truth. You may not see it right away, but if you keep on speaking God's Word, standing on His promises in faith, it will happen. You will become what you speak. (2 Cor. 5:17)Your entire life will be transformed. (Rom. 12:2, Is. 40:29, 2 Cor. 12:9, Ps. 107:20, Hos. 5:15)

As transformation comes, be careful not to return to whatever God freed you from. (Gal. 5:1) If doubt or unbelief try to overtake you, know that it is not from God. Speak out what God says. Don't allow yourself to think or speak anything negative. Stand on (and speak) God's Word.

"Now may the God of hope fill you with all joy and peace in believing, that you may abound in hope by the power of the Holy Spirit." Rom. 15:13

I pray this devotional will strengthen and encourage you as you walk out the new life and plan God has for you (Jer. 29:11). These scriptures have transformed my thoughts, renewed my mind and therefore transformed my life. I am praying for you as you make this journey with Jesus. Each day there will be a spoken confession of your identity in Christ (the big words at the top of the page) and a Scripture for meditation and memorization, if you would like. Allow the truth to transform you and the Word to bring new life to your bones, as you discover who God created you to be.

PRAYER OF SALVATION

"...if you confess with your mouth the Lord Jesus and believe in your heart that God raised Him from the dead, you will be saved. For with the heart, one believes unto righteousness, and with the mouth confession is made unto salvation." Romans 10:9-10

"For whoever calls on the Name of the Lord shall be saved." Romans 10:13

The first step to living in all the fullness of God is salvation. Pray this prayer out loud:

"Father God, I come to you in the Name of Jesus. I confess that I am a sinner. I believe that Your Son, Jesus Christ, died for the forgiveness of my sins and rose from the dead for my victory. Please forgive me of all my sins. I repent of anything that is not pleasing to You. Jesus, come into my heart as my Lord and Savior. I surrender my life to you. I ask You to fill me with Your Spirit. I confess that Jesus Christ is Lord of my life. In Jesus' Name, Amen."

"I say to you that likewise there will be more joy in Heaven over one sinner who repents than over ninety-nine just persons who need no repentance."Luke 15:7

I AM CREATED IN GOD'S IMAGE

*"So **God created man in His own image**; in the image of God He created him; **male and female** He created them."Genesis 1:27*

People are born with an intrinsic yearning for 4 things- identity, purpose, acceptance, and love. God created you in His own image, so your true identity is in *His* identity. God defines the Truth of who you are and how you relate to Him in His Word. God is made up of 3 parts- the Father (mind/thoughts), the Holy Spirit (emotions/feelings/intuition), and the Son (physical body). We can all easily identify ourselves in this way. Humans are spirit, we have a soul, and live in a body. (1 Thes. 5:23) Until I really knew God, though, my identity was wrapped up in what I did, what I had, who I knew, what I looked like, how much money I had or didn't have, where I worked. No matter what it looked like on the outside, my self-

21

esteem and self-worth were catastrophically suffering. Sin distorts the originally created image, but Christ makes restoration of that image possible. When you are born again, you die spiritually. Galatians 2:20 says, "…it is no longer I who live, but Christ lives in me." The phrase "finding yourself" becomes an oxymoron, because it is only in losing yourself and finding Christ that you can ever really know who you are. You have to know who Christ is.

GOD GIVES ME POWER TO GET WEALTH

*"And you shall remember the Lord your God, for **it is He who gives you power to get wealth** that He may establish His covenant which He swore to your fathers, as it is this day." Deuteronomy 8:18*

In the verse right before this one, it says, "...then you say in your heart, '*My* power and the might of *my* hand have gained me this wealth." (Deut. 8:17) There are no "self-made" fortunes. James 1:17 says, "Every good gift and every perfect gift is from above..." Acknowledging God's provision, giving Him the credit, and being grateful to Him for His blessings are key factors in experiencing an outpouring of His abundance. Notice the verse above doesn't say that He gives you wealth. It says that He gives you the *power* to get wealth. Ideas, open doors, divine opportunities, funding, creative solutions. What has God called you to do? What do you have a passion for? What do you do that no one else can do quite like you? What makes you stand out? Ask God to reveal *His* plans and purpose for your life. Whatever your calling is, know that where God guides, He provides, *that He may establish His covenant.* God gives wealth to those who can be trusted to purposely finance the advancement of His Kingdom. This is where the kingdom of self is overthrown. (Mt. 16:24-25) The Bible teaches us that we are to seek God first (Mt. 6:33), to love God with all our heart, soul, mind, and strength (Mk. 12:30), and to love others (Mk. 12:31). Using our gifts, talents, and money for others, rather than for personal fulfillment, tears down the walls of self and lays the foundation for love, which is the ultimate wealth of God's Kingdom.

I AM A SPECIAL TREASURE

"For you are a holy people to the Lord your God, and the Lord has chosen you to be a people for Himself, **a special treasure** *above all the peoples who are on the face of the earth." Deuteronomy 14:2*

If you have ever, at any time in your life, thought that you were no different than anyone else, think again. As a born again child of the Most High God you are holy, meaning that you are consecrated, set apart, blessed, by God Himself, the King of Kings and Lord of Lords. He has chosen *you*, appointed *you*, as a special treasure, a peculiar people, a part of His very own tribe, a sheep of His flock, above all the other people on the face of the earth that ever was or ever will be. You were called to be a minister of reconciliation, bringing others into the fold. (2 Cor. 5:18-19) You were appointed to be a light to others, that they may see your good works and glorify God. (Mt. 5:16) You were chosen to feed the hungry, clothe the poor, comfort the sick, give hope to those in prison. (Mt. 25:31-40) Your voice was singled out to pray for others, for nations, for the Kingdom of

God to be established on earth. (Ez. 22:30) You have to stay close to God, in His Word, in prayer, in worship, listening for His voice. You have to learn His ways. And you have to live them because *that* is who you are. I love how Ezekiel 16:13 says, "You were exceedingly beautiful, and succeeded to royalty." Royalty doesn't live the same as everyone else. Elevation requires separation, and costly treasure is kept in a special, safe place, not in the barn out back. Treasure is brilliant. Light reflects off diamonds and gold, revealing a brilliant reflection. When you look at your reflection, do you see yourself as the child of the King of glory? That's your true self, the person God created you to be, His special treasure.

I AM OBEDIENT

*"Now it shall come to pass, if you **diligently obey the voice of the Lord your God**, to observe carefully all His commands which I command you today, that the Lord your God will set you high above all nations of the earth." Deuteronomy 28:1*

The only way we can nail our own flesh to the Cross is by submitting to the One who died on it. Obedience isn't what you do for God. It's what you do as a result of what Christ has done for you. Obedience doesn't earn God's love or salvation, but it is visible evidence of what's in your heart. It's the mark on your forehead that you belong to Jesus. Obedience isn't just about doing right. It's about *believing* right. It's about pursuing God and *His* righteousness. It's who you are and Whose you are. It's noticeable in the words you speak, what you spend your time and money on, how you dress, where you hang out. It's reflecting the goodness of God in your life so that others will see your light and be drawn to it. I remember a time when I thought I was so far gone, that there was no coming back. I had no hope, until I saw what God had done in someone else's life and I knew that if He could save *her*, there was still hope for me. There are very real forces fighting against us (1 Jn. 2) to distract us from the assignment God has given each one of us. Obedience is a powerful weapon against the forces of darkness. You were anointed (commissioned) for a specific assignment (1 Jn. 2:27) that no one but you can accomplish. That's why the devil wants to distract, deceive, and discourage you and why Paul says, "For the good that I will to do, I do not do; but the evil I will not to do, that I practice. Now if I do what I will not to do, it is no longer I who do it, but sin that dwells in me." (Rom. 7:19-20) Your obedience is your weapon. (1 Sam. 15:22-23)

I AM SET HIGH ABOVE ALL NATIONS OF THE EARTH

"Now it shall come to pass, if you diligently obey the voice of the Lord your God, to observe carefully all His commands which I command you today, that the Lord your God will **set you high above all nations of the earth.***" Deuteronomy 28:1*

Notice the verse says "if". God is saying that *if* you do this, *then* He will do that. The blessings of obedience are listed in Deuteronomy 28:3-13. God says that if you will obey His commandments, He will pour out His blessings on you with such force that they will "come upon you and overtake you." *They will chase you down.* They will be inescapable. You will be blessed wherever you are. Your children will be blessed. Your work will be blessed. Your investments will be blessed. Your food will be blessed. You will be blessed in your coming and going. You will be blessed in warfare. Everything you own will be blessed. Everything you do will be blessed. Your home will be blessed. Your name will be blessed. You will be set apart as one of God's holy people. You will be blessed with abundance. You will be a lender and not a borrower. God guarantees to uphold this Word because it's His covenant (or contract) with His people. In honoring His covenant, He is glorified and you are established as one of His own.

I AM BLESSED WHEREVER I AM

"Blessed shall you be in the city, and blessed shall you be in the country." Deuteronomy 28:3

Genesis 39:21-23 tells of Joseph, whose brothers sold him into slavery, being in prison after he was falsely accused of sexual advances against the wife of Potiphar, one of the Pharaoh's chief officers. Even in that situation, God blessed Joseph, making him overseer of the prison. After interpreting dreams for two of the inmates, he was asked to interpret a dream for the Pharaoh himself. God gave Joseph favor with the Pharaoh and was put in charge of all Pharaoh had. Joseph was second only to Pharaoh in all the land of Egypt. A lot of people would say that Joseph was a lucky man, but the Bible says that he was *blessed*. God is sovereign. He is in complete control of *everything and everybody*. Deuteronomy 28:3 means that no matter where you are, what it looks or feels like, no matter what people say, if you diligently obey God's commandments - *you are blessed*. You're better off living in a war zone with the blessing of God on your life than you are living under the curse

of disobedience anywhere else on earth. (Deut. 28:15-
68)

I AM BLESSED IN THE FRUIT OF MY BODY

*"**Blessed shall be the fruit of your body**, the produce of your ground and the increase of your herds, the increase of your cattle and the offspring of your flocks." Deuteronomy 28:4*

The fruit of your body literally refers to your children. Because of *your* obedience, your children are blessed. Your ability to become pregnant is blessed. The produce of your ground refers to where you sow your seed- the place where you make your living, such as your job. Your work will be of excellent quality and increased production. The produce of your ground also means the place where you plant your seed. That would be where you give tithes and offerings. When you sow an offering, name that seed. Say, "I'm sowing this seed for _____, in faith, in the Name of Jesus." And make sure you are sowing into fertile ground. Your words are seeds, too, so speak life. (Prov. 18:21) Your herds are your family, friends, and other associations. Your cattle refer to your provision. Deuteronomy 28:11 says, "And the Lord will grant you plenty of goods, in the fruit of your body, in the increase of your livestock, and in the produce of your ground..." Where does your prosperity come from? You already know! "For every beast of the forest is Mine, and the cattle on a thousand hills." (Ps. 50:10) He is able to make all grace abound toward you. (2 Cor. 9:8) Your flocks refer to your personal ministry.

Every believer is a minister. (Col. 1:25) You are called to bring others to Christ, to help the poor, to bring freedom to those in chains, to preach, to teach, to heal the sick, to cast out demons, to share the love of God everywhere you go with everyone you encounter, to give hope to the lost, a listening ear to the lonely. You are blessed *to be a blessing.*

I AM BLESSED COMING IN AND BLESSED GOING OUT

"Blessed shall you be when you come in and blessed shall you be when you go out." Deuteronomy 28:6

Who watches over your family and your home while you're at work or out running errands? I mean, if you aren't there to make sure everything is safe and protected, then who is? How can you even concentrate on what you're doing, without worrying over what could be happening without you there to keep things running smooth? How can you be expected to perform at top level while you're on your job or driving or in the drive-thru getting espresso, when your family and home are left unattended, at the risk of all kinds of peril and danger? Deuteronomy 28:6 is God's covenant promise of protection for your family and property. It's also His protection for you when you leave your property. Your journey will be blessed. Your endeavors and labor will be blessed. It's like having a supernatural security force. It is God who goes out before you and God who brings you in. (Num. 27:17) You are led by God, every time you leave your home or come back to it. Psalm 121:8 says, *"The Lord shall preserve your going out and your coming in from this time forth, and even forevermore."* When you come home at the end of the day, your house will still be standing. Your kids will be safe.

Maybe not angelic, but safe. You can focus on being the best God has called you to be, in whatever He has called you to do. You are under God's direction and protection.

MY ENEMIES FLEE BEFORE MY FACE

*"The Lord will cause **your enemies who rise against you to be defeated before your face**; they shall come out against you one way and flee before you seven ways." Deuteronomy 28:7*

When someone seems to be an enemy to you, don't fight the person. ((2 Cor. 10:4-5) The real enemy is Satan and he uses demons to attack the children of God. (Eph. 6:10-13) Demons often use a person to do their evil works through. That doesn't mean the person is possessed, but they can still be used if they've left a spiritual door open through sin, unforgiveness, unrepentance, or other works of the flesh. (Gal. 5:19-21) The forces of darkness can't stand in the presence of Jesus. Jesus is alive inside of *you*. (Gal. 2:20, 2 Cor. 13:5) At the Name of Jesus, *every* knee must bow, of those in Heaven, and of those on earth. (Php. 2:10) Deuteronomy 28:7 is one of the covenant blessings of obedience. Remember, God honors His covenant even above His Name. (Ps. 138:2) Your obedience to God's commandments assures you of His protection in the face of attack. You don't have to put up with the enemy coming against you anymore. He may try, but God is your Defender. (Ps. 62:5-8) All you have to do is call out to Him. Start rebuking that thing, binding it up, casting it at the feet of Jesus! I love how Psalm 18 describes God responding to our crying out to Him. I can picture Him getting a phone call and saying, "They did *what* to My baby?!" and jumping on His cloud, throwing lightening everywhere, on His way to burn them up with the breath of His nostrils. He does that for me all the time! And He does it like that for you, too.

MY STOREHOUSES ARE BLESSED

"The Lord will command the blessing on you in your storehouses and in all to which you set your hand, and He will bless you in the land which the Lord your God is giving you." Deuteronomy 28:8

Your storehouse is the place where you store up for the future. Your savings account, your investments, your 401k. It could be your food pantry, your emergency supplies, your cleaning supplies, your office supplies. God blessed obedience in this way so that when hard times come, those who do not have enough can be blessed also. Divine doors open up for you to minister to the needs of others. Your storehouse is also your local church. Malachi 3:10 says, "Bring all the tithes into the storehouse, that there may be food in My house, and try Me now in this," says the Lord of hosts, "if I will not open for you the windows of Heaven and pour out for you such blessing that there will not be room enough to receive it." God said "try Me". That's a pretty strong statement, but He means it. My brother told me once, "I used to think I couldn't afford to pay tithes, but I know now that I can't afford not to." You see, when you give the first 10 percent of your income as a tithe, "somehow", even though your bills add up to this much, and you only have that much, your bills will be paid and you'll still have money left over, even though it doesn't add up on paper and there's no logical explanation for it.

Any offering you give above the tithe is also going into the storehouse. Again, always name your seed and speak to it. "I am sowing this seed into _____, in faith, in the Name of Jesus." God especially blesses us when we sow into the advancement of His Kingdom, which includes His purposes and will upon the earth. Feeding the poor, supporting missionaries, clothing drives for the homeless, prison ministry, hospital and hospice ministry, youth ministry, evangelism. It takes money to minister.

I AM BLESSED IN ALL I SET MY HAND TO

"The Lord will command the blessing on you in your storehouses and in all to which you set your hand, and He will bless you in the land which the Lord your God is giving you." Deuteronomy 28:8

Notice the words *"in all to which you set your hand"*. First, the word "all" means all, everything. Next, it says "you". Things that *you* do. Then the word "set". That implies something fixed, not something that you do once and move on to do something else and wonder why the first thing you did wasn't blessed. Anything, everything, all things that you, yourself, do diligently, consistently, patiently, expectantly, God will cause to be supernaturally blessed, above and beyond the standard for that thing, because you obey His commandments. My cousin, who was the one that helped me learn about the things of God when I was a newborn Christian, had a tomato plant at the end of the house. She prayed over it a lot and we both were doing everything we knew to do to walk in God's ways and in His Presence. We lived and breathed God's Spirit. A tomato plant seems like such an insignificant thing in the things of the Spirit, but God blessed that tomato plant. Seriously. I'm from the south. I've grown up around tomato plants every summer since as far back as I can remember, and I have never seen a tomato plant *taller than a house.* That one was. And always full of tomatoes. Nothing is insignificant in all of God's creation. *Your obedience* is blessed in all that you do so that others will see God's hand and reach out for it.

I AM BLESSED IN THE LAND THE LORD MY GOD IS GIVING ME

*"The Lord will command the blessing on you in your storehouses and in all to which you set your hand, and **He will bless you in the land which the Lord your God is giving you.**" Deuteronomy 28:8*

The word "land" here means exactly that, land. The Bible talks a lot about the Promised Land. It's real land, but it's a spiritual place. It doesn't refer to Heaven. What you must know, is that everything in the physical also has an unseen, spiritual entity that is more real than anything you can see or touch. Because it is spiritual, it is therefore eternal and much more real. God can most definitely give you land as part of the covenant blessing He has for you, even if you can't begin to wrap your mind around how that could happen, but what I want to focus on is the Promised Land. Before you became a Christian, you were living in a spiritual place the Bible refers to as the wilderness. Once you were filled with the Spirit of Jesus, you began your journey into the Promised Land. Just like God was with Moses and Joshua, leading His people out of slavery in Egypt, he is with you on your journey out of the slavery of sin and oppression. It took the Israelites 40 years to make their journey. It should've only taken 11 days. Sin and fear kept God from allowing them to enter. (Num. 14:32-34) Things happen along the way. You're in unfamiliar territory. You're tired. You find yourself in warfare. You aren't sure if you're even going in the right direction. You often find yourself standing right in the middle of the enemy's camp. What are you going to DO?? Trust God. Follow His marching orders (commandments). God goes before you to lead you and comes behind you as your rear guard. Your faith and obedience are your most effective weapons. Don't fear and don't let go, because God would never give you something that He knows you can't get.

I AM ESTABLISHED AS ONE OF GOD'S OWN HOLY PEOPLE

*"**The Lord will establish you as a holy people to Himself**, just as He has sworn to you, if you keep the commandments of the Lord your God and walk in His ways." Deuteronomy 28:9*

The word "establish" here means to maintain or raise up to a permanent place of never ending status. Notice this verse says, "He has *sworn* to you." Not only is God incapable of lying, (Titus 1:2) He even goes a step further and *swears* on this promise. By saying that He will establish you as a holy people to Himself, He is saying that He will set you up, help you, strengthen you as *His* people, you will be *sacred* to Him, a member of *His* Royal family. If the king of the wealthiest country in the world saw you living in a Section 8 government housing project and extended his love and compassion to you and put you in a palace, fully furnished with the best that money could buy, with housekeepers and cooks and someone to drive you around wherever you wanted to go, in a luxury vehicle, and gave you clothes and jewelry and expensive perfumes, that king would be taking you in as his own family, adopting you. That king would expect you to act like one of his family. His love for you would desire for you to conform to a higher standard of living, for your *own* sake. The king would also expect your loyalty and dedication for giving you a better life. That's how it is with God. You are spiritually destitute until He adopts you. All He asks you to do is follow His instructions and trust Him. Your dedication and obedience prove to Him what's really in your heart. That's what makes you holy. That's what makes you His.

I AM CALLED BY THE NAME OF THE LORD

*"Then all peoples of the earth shall see that **you are called by the Name of the Lord,** and they shall be afraid of you."* Deuteronomy 28:10

God's Name becomes a part of who you are. It means that He is your Protector, your Provider, your Healer, your Sustainer, your Teacher, your Defender, your Everything. It means He takes care of you in every way, just like a parent does for their child. Your Father is the King of Kings. There is none higher. I've been called by a lot of names in my life- Poor, Stupid, Fat, Ugly, Failure. And those are the nicer ones. When I first became a child of God, I was still called by the names Inmate, Addict, Homeless, Broken, Angry, Depressed, Outcast, Whore, Damaged. Although I was fully adopted by God and accepted as if I were His own, I was new to God's family and it took a while for me to learn how my new family did things. People didn't recognize my new identity right away. I had to spend time with my Father before I started to take on His characteristics and walk in His ways without falling down every few steps. Just like a baby learning to walk, Father God would help me get back up and try again. He encouraged me to keep on trying and to trust Him. There were lots of times I would think "I can't do this" or "I know I'm going to mess this up", but I know now that a lot of that was the enemy's voice. He speaks to us in *our own voice*, through our thoughts, so that we will think it's our own thought and add more self-defeating thoughts to it. Once we buy into the doubt, discouragement, distraction, and deception, he's got us. Silence that voice with your Father's voice- "I can do *all* things through Christ, who strengthens me." (Php. 4:13) "Greater is He that is in me, than he who is in the world." (1 Jn. 4:4) Romans 8:14-15 says, "For as many as are led by the Spirit of God, these are the sons (and daughters) of God. For you did not receive the spirit of bondage again to fear, but you received the Spirit of adoption by whom we cry out, Abba, Father." You are *God's* child now.

I AM STRONG

*"**Be strong** and of good courage; do not fear nor be afraid of them; for the Lord your God, He is one who goes with you, He will not leave you nor forsake you." Deuteronomy 31:6*

The Hebrew word for "strong" in this verse means to seize, along with be constant, continue, and encourage. What God is saying here is that you need to grab hold of His Word and hang on for dear life. The Word of God is living and powerful, sharper than any two edged sword. (Heb. 4:12) God will supply *all* of your needs, according to *His* riches in glory, by Christ Jesus. (Php. 4:19) The Passion Translation of Hebrews 10:23-25 says, "So now we must cling tightly to the hope that lives within us, knowing that God always keeps His promises! Discover creative ways to encourage others and to motivate them toward acts of compassion, doing beautiful works as expressions of love. This is not the time to pull away and neglect meeting together as some have formed the habit of doing, because we need each other! In fact, we should come together even more frequently, eager to encourage and urge each other onward as we anticipate that day dawning." There is strength in numbers. You are not alone. Even if you have to encourage yourself, encourage yourself in what the Word says about you. Jesus Christ is *the Living Word of God*! When you encourage yourself in the Word, Christ

Himself is with you. (Jn. 1:1) Being strong means pushing through the pain, the heartache, the feeling of being overwhelmed, and knowing that God is in control. Isaiah 35:4 (NLT) says, "Say to those who are afraid, "Be strong, and do not fear, for your God is coming to destroy your enemies. He is coming to save you."" You are so much stronger than you think because your strength comes from the Lord. (Is. 40:31)

I AM COURAGEOUS

*"Be strong and **of good courage;** do not fear nor be afraid of them; for the Lord your God, He is one who goes with you. He will not leave you nor forsake you." Deuteronomy 31:6*

Fear is a state of mind that brings physical paralysis to one's ability to take action. Fear is a curse of disobedience. (Deut. 28:65-67) You are redeemed from the curse. (Gal. 3:13) The Hebrew word for "courage" in this verse means to be alert, steadfastly minded, to be stronger, established. It means to stay intentionally focused and stand firm. What is something that you've always wanted to do, but thought that you couldn't? You can do it, whatever it is. I used to live in constant fear, worry, and dread. Defeat was my sole expectation, no matter what the situation was. Matthew 19:26 says, "With God, *all* things are possible." That's a promise. 2 Corinthians 1:20 (NIV) says, "For no matter how many promises God has made, they are "Yes" in Christ." Philippians 4:13 says, "I can do *all* things through Christ who strengthens me." Notice that says, "*I can*", not "He will". You're going to have to get off your blessed assurance and do the thing that needs to be done, chipping away at it day after day, not giving up, not giving in to the doubts or fears when they rise up. Just keep moving forward, holding on to God, giving Him praise, asking for His guidance. Proverbs 16:3 says, "Commit your works to the Lord, and your thoughts will be established." Whatever you're doing, commit it to God, for His glory. When you commit yourself to following God's commandments and walking in His ways, He promises to prosper all that you set our hand to do. (Deut. 28:8) God is all powerful and He fights for you. (Jer. 20:11) You *can* do what you've always dreamed of.

I DO NOT FEAR

*"Be strong and of good courage; **do not fear** nor be afraid of them; for the Lord your God, He is one who goes with you. He will not leave you nor forsake you." Deuteronomy 31:6*

Fear is the opposite of faith. Fear is a demonic spirit. (2 Tim. 1:7) It's one of the devil's most effective tools used to kill, steal, and destroy. (Jn. 10:10) Faith is a spiritual force. According to 2 Corinthians 4:13, "And since we have the same *spirit of faith, according to what is written, "I believed, and therefore I spoke.""* In other words, God's Word + your belief + speaking the Word out of your mouth = FAITH. I used to be crippled by fear, the unsubstantiated "what if" and "I can't" dress rehearsals that were forever going on in my mental theater. What was going on in my mind arrested my life. At some point, I realized that I had allowed fear to bury me in addiction, and that because of that I had lost every person in my life that I had ever loved, and that loved me. I didn't think I had any reason for living anymore. I had nothing and nobody left to lose, so I chose to live. I ate the Word, morning, noon, and night. I spoke God's Word in the face of fear, and I kept speaking it, no matter what I thought or what things felt like. Eventually, the way I responded to fear changed. I believed. When fear tried to raise its ugly little head, I had to deal with it one way or the other, so I determined to face it. I looked fear dead in the eye every single time and annihilated it by speaking the Word of God. OUT LOUD. Don't miss that part. Faith comes by *hearing*, and hearing by *the Word of God*. (Rom. 10:17) Read. Trust and believe. Speak. Conquer.

I AM NOT AFRAID

*"Be strong and of good courage; do not fear **nor be afraid of them**; for the Lord your God, He is one who goes with you. He will not leave you nor forsake you." Deuteronomy 31:6*

The Contemporary English Version of Psalm 118:5-6 says, "When I was really hurting, I prayed to the Lord. He answered my prayer, and took my worries away. The Lord is on my side, and I am not afraid of what others can do to me." The Hebrew word for afraid here means to be in awe of, harassed, terrified. The Bible doesn't say that things like that won't happen. It says don't allow them to overwhelm you with fear and don't allow them to continue. Stop fear dead in its tracks, knowing that the Lord is fighting for you, that He will never leave you alone, and He will never give up on you or turn you away. (Rom. 8:38-39) Trust in God and don't try to figure things out for yourself. (Prov. 3:5-6) One of the last things my mother ever said to me was, "There are some things you'll never know the answer to, but God does." She meant that even when I didn't understand why things were they way they were, God knew and I should trust Him and take rest in that. Isaiah 12:2 says, "Behold, God is my salvation, I will trust and not be afraid." And in Mark 5:36, Jesus says, "Do not be afraid; only believe." When you try to figure things out and fix everything yourself, you're not trusting God. You're trying to take the place of God. You've got to get out of the way! Trust God to be God! Paul says in Philippians 4:6, "Be anxious for *nothing*, but in *everything* by prayer and supplication, *with thanksgiving*, let your requests be made known to God." That means *ask* and thank Him, knowing that *it is already done*.

THE LORD GOD GOES WITH ME

*"Be strong and of good courage; do not fear nor be afraid of them; for **the Lord your God, He is one who goes with you**. He will not leave you nor forsake you." Deuteronomy 31:6*

Your best position in the face of adversity is "I can't, but God can." (2 Cor. 12:9) At 55 years old, I came alive. I've survived every kind of abuse you can name. I've been locked up, addicted to drugs for over 40 years, in a coma & on life support for spinal meningitis and a brain infection, which caused so much stress on my body that I suffered a stroke. I was homeless for years, literally living on the streets. I was abandoned as a child. But God was with me. He fought for me, my entire life. I didn't know it then, but I know it now. After I got out of the hospital, I was tormented by the demons that had visited me while I was in the coma. I couldn't make sense of anything. I couldn't use my body. It felt like my brain had been rearranged. I stayed in bed for about a month, trying to will myself to die. I was angry that it didn't happen. I pushed people away that were just there to check on me. Thank God, they prayed for me anyway. I finally dragged myself up and started confessing God's Word. Every day. No matter what. I knew it was the only hope I had of living. I hated it, but I made myself do it. It hasn't even been a full year since then, but I did my first 5k. I haven't had so much as a common cold, and I have no signs whatsoever of stroke or illness, other than a couple of scars. That's because the same power that lives in me is the same power that raised Jesus Christ from the dead. (Rom. 8:11, Eph. 1:19-21, 1 Jn. 4:4) That same power is in *you*, to do exceedingly, abundantly above *all* that you ask or think. (Eph. 3:20) That's the power of God, living inside of *you*.

I AM NOT ALONE

*"Be strong and of good courage; do not fear nor be afraid of them; for the Lord your God, He is one who goes with you. **He will not leave you** nor forsake you."* Deuteronomy 31:6

The Promised Land is the land you enter when you make the choice to believe God. As soon as you intentionally choose to believe God and follow His commandments, you've set out on the journey. In Joshua chapter 1, God told Joshua to lead the Israelites across the Jordan River, into the Promised Land. In verse 5, the Lord told Joshua, "No man shall be able to stand before you all the days of your life; *as I was with Moses, so I will be with you. I will not leave you or forsake you.*" In verse 9 God tells Joshua again, "Have I not **commanded** you? Be strong and of good courage; do not be afraid, nor be dismayed, for *the Lord your God is with you **wherever** you go.*" Notice in verse 8, there's a condition. "This Book of the Law shall not depart from *your mouth*, but you shall **meditate in it** day and night, that you may observe **to *do*** according to *all* that is written in it. For ***then*** *you will make your way prosperous, and **then** you will have good success.*" Speaking the Word, meditating on it, and living it out in obedience is how you get to the Promised Land. (Josh. 1:8-9) Isaiah 43:2 says, "When you pass through the waters, I will be with you; And through the rivers, they shall not overflow you. When you walk through the fire, you shall not be burned, nor shall the flame scorch you." It doesn't say "if", it says "when". There will be difficulties along the way, but God is with you. When Shadrach, Meshach, and Abednego were thrown into the fiery furnace, King Nebuchadnezzar looked into the furnace and said, "I see four men loose, walking in the midst of the fire; and they are not hurt, and the form of the fourth is like the Son of God." (Dan. 3:25) They didn't even smell like smoke! Neither will you.

I AM NOT FORSAKEN

*"Be strong and of good courage; do not fear nor be afraid of them; for the Lord your God, He is one who goes with you. He will not leave you **nor forsake you.**" Deuteronomy 31:6*

Forsaken means abandoned or deserted. Rejected. Rejection is a destructive ruling spirit with deep roots that affect a person's entire life negatively. When I first started looking into it, I found that every problem I had ever encountered stemmed from the root of rejection. When a child is not shown love *appropriately or adequately*, it opens the door for the spirit of rejection to enter, thereby affecting the person's ability to give and receive love. Throughout that person's life, the spirit manifests itself in such a way that it seems like the problem lies elsewhere, (addiction, eating disorders, mental illness, sexual deviance, violence, etc.) so the real problem goes undetected and never gets dealt with. The *root* of the problem, the *real problem*, is the spirit of rejection. Isaiah 49:15 says, "Can a woman forget her nursing child, and not have compassion on the son of her womb? Surely they may forget, yet I will not forget you." Jesus was despised and rejected by men, a Man of sorrows and acquainted with grief. (Is. 53:3) Jesus' own people rejected Him. (Jn. 1:11) When we respond to life with strong faith in God, it serves as a good, hard punch in the devil's mouth. God promises you, in 1

Samuel 12:22, that He will not forsake you, for His Name's sake, because it *pleased Him* to make you *His own.* And in Isaiah 42:16, "I will bring the blind by a way they did not know; I will lead them in paths they have not known. I will make darkness light before them, and crooked places straight. These things I will do for them, and not forsake them." Jesus was rejected so that *you* could be accepted, not merely as an adopted orphan, but as a legitimate, beloved heir to the Kingdom.

I AM BEAUTIFUL TO GOD

*"But the Lord said to Samuel, "Do not look at his appearance or his stature, because I have refused him. For **the Lord does not see as man sees; for man looks at the outward appearance, but the Lord looks at the heart."** 1 Samuel 16:7*

God created you in His own image. (Gen. 1:27) God is a Spirit, so when He looks at you, He looks at your spirit, your inner self. Your spirit is the *real* you. We are all spirits living in physical bodies, kind of like a priceless gift wrapped in a cardboard box. The wrapping can be pretty, but at best, it's still just a box. The good stuff, the thing of value, is *inside* the box. Do you spend more time, money, thought, attention, and effort on the box and its wrapping or on the gift inside? Your heart is where the springs of life flow from. (Prov. 4:23) God says in His Word that purity, obedience, trust in Him, repentance, love, righteousness, holiness, praise, compassion, generosity, commitment, the desire to seek after Him, faithfulness, forgiveness, and sharing the Gospel are beautiful to Him. All those things come from the heart. You can't buy those things. You can't wear them. No one else can give them to you. They're *inside of you*. The fruit of the Spirit (the resulting evidence of the Holy Spirit's presence inside of you) is love, joy, peace, longsuffering, kindness, goodness, faithfulness, gentleness, and self control. (Gal. 5:22-23)

Those are implanted in you by the Holy Spirit. The more you spend time reading the Word and applying it to your life, the more that fruit grows and matures. You will sow those same seeds into others, and produce fruit in their lives. Isaiah 58:11 says, "You shall be like a watered garden, and like a spring of water, whose waters do not fail." The more of God that He sees in *you*, the more He finds you beautiful, and so do others. My prayer is that you will see that, too.

I PROSPER IN ALL THAT I DO

"He shall be like a tree planted by the rivers of water that brings forth its fruit in its season, whose leaf also shall not wither; and **whatever he does shall prosper."** *Psalm 1:3*

This verse likens the person who delights in and meditates on the Word of God to a tree. The word "planted" is actually "transplanted" in Hebrew. The person that delights in the Word and really spends their time thinking on it, is like a tree *transplanted* by the rivers. In other words, they are *intentionally planted there from somewhere else*, into a place where they will be nourished by rivers of water. Not just one river. Rivers. In John 7:38-39, Jesus describes the indwelling of the Holy Spirit as "rivers of living water." Water is symbolic of the Holy Spirit. Spending time reading and meditating on the Word is time spent with the Holy Spirit. You can't help but grow, increase and prosper. Your environment influences your thinking. Your thinking affects your emotions. Your emotions determine your choices. Whatever you give your time and attention to determines your life. The word "prosper" means to do well or succeed in life; to succeed, thrive, grow, flourish, in a vigorous way. To prosper means to move forward. When the Holy Spirit pushes you forward, it's with supernatural force. What does that mean as far as who you are? It means that you are someone that lives according to God's Word rather than someone who lives like the rest of the world. It means you intentionally make choices that reflect God's ways and His Word in your life, and God gives you His promise to prosper your life. *You* will be blessed. Your *children* will be blessed. *Their children* will be blessed, because of *you*.

I AM SET APART

*"But know that **the Lord has set apart for Himself** him who is godly; the Lord will hear when I call to Him." Psalm 4:3*

When God sets you apart, He is giving you an order to separate yourself and your ways from those of the world (unbelievers) for a specific purpose, a job that He's giving to *you*. He's giving you a calling, the one that He created you and you alone to fulfill. When you are set apart, you are holy, sacred to God. That doesn't mean you're supposed to go into exile or be self-righteous. Just because you live and work in the world doesn't mean that you're of this world. (Jn. 17:16) It means that you are supposed to live in such a way as to be uniquely different from others around you and focused on a specific purpose. Two hints- "godly" and "the Lord will hear when I call to Him". You are set apart to live like a child of the King. You have to make the choice to do that. Ask God what His purpose for your life is. Then, dig into His Word. Certain things will jump out at you. Maybe even things that you've read before, that didn't really mean anything at the time, but all of a sudden hit you like a ton of bricks. Oh, yeahhhhh! Praise God! And that's something else... Worship will take you straight into the King's presence. His glory will rise up over you, surround you, and you will have visions, revelations, you'll start seeing God everywhere in everything. You'll *get it*. How can I be so sure? Look at the ending of Psalm 4:3 again. *The Lord will hear you when you call to Him.* See, He's waiting for you right now!

I AM GODLY

*"But know that the Lord has set apart for Himself **him who is godly**; the Lord will hear when I call to Him." Psalm 4:3*

The word "godly" refers to purity and righteousness, but it also means "devoted to God". It's a relationship with God that produces actions that are pleasing to Him. Jeremiah 29:13 says, "And you will seek Me and find Me, when you search for Me with all your heart." The word "heart" here is "mind, will, and emotions". It's your total being. When you hunger and thirst for God, when you seek Him with all your heart, He takes notice. (Ps. 37:4) When you conform to His ways, He moves on your behalf. (Ps. 84:11) When you pray, He answers you. (Jms. 5:16) God doesn't expect perfection. Romans 3:10-11 says, "There is none righteous, no, not one; There is none who understands; There is none who seeks after God." Our righteousness is in Christ alone, (1 Cor. 1:30) but in Romans 4:3 it says, "Abraham *believed God*, and it was accounted to him for *righteousness*." Belief is a choice. Again, you *must* spend time and attention in the Word. What you focus on goes into your heart and comes out of your mouth. *You are godly*. You are devoted to God. You are devoted to spending time in His Word and applying it to your life. That's wisdom and understanding. You are faithful in seeking Him and serving Him. You *believe Him* and He accounts that as *your* righteousness.

THE LORD HEARS WHEN I CALL TO HIM

"But know that the Lord has set apart for Himself him who is godly;
the Lord will hear when I call to Him." *Psalm 4:3*

If your child were in trouble and cried out to you, would you respond? Of course you would, even if that child had thrown a temper tantrum or poured paint on your new car or skipped school. No matter what, that's your child. That's how Father God is with you, too. It's easy to think you've done some bad things, so He won't listen to you, much less help, but God is the *perfect* Father. His love is completely unconditional, expecting nothing in return. God not only forgives, *He forgets*. (Jer. 31:34) There's no reason to hide, because you can't, anyway. (Ps. 139:12-14) If you feel like there's something you've done to hinder your prayers, ask God to forgive you and move on, but don't stop talking to Him. Prayerlessness is powerlessness. God wants to bless you. He wants to guide you into the best that this life has to offer. Jeremiah 29:11-12 says, "For I know the thoughts that I think toward you, says the Lord, thoughts of peace and not of evil, to give you a future and a hope. Then you will call upon Me and go and pray to Me, *and I will listen to you*." That doesn't have any "ifs" or "buts" in there, does it? Prayers don't have to be long, drawn out, eloquent, thee, thy, and thou laden speeches. 1 Thessalonians 5:17 says, "Pray without ceasing." I keep a running conversation in my head all day long. I have prayer time also, but I constantly talk to God throughout my

71

day. I even talk to Him when I wake up in the middle of the night to go to the bathroom or get a drink. He's a friend who sticks closer than a brother. (Prov. 18:24) There's nothing God doesn't already know about you. He even knows things *you* don't know about yourself. Philippians 4:6 says, "Be anxious for *nothing*, but in *everything* by prayer and supplication, *with thanksgiving*, let your requests be made known to God." Your Father God hears *you*.

I PRAY TO GOD IN THE MORNING

"My voice You shall hear in the morning, O Lord in the morning I will direct it to You, and I will look up." Psalm 5:3

The Bible tells us to pray without ceasing (1 Thes. 5:17), to pray about everything (Php. 4:6-7), and not to give up (Lk. 18:1). Morning prayer is time set aside specifically for prayer. (Ps. 88:13) Here's a list of reasons why morning prayer is so important:

- You honor God by giving Him first priority (Col. 1:18)
- You love & desire God and you *want* to spend time with Him (Prov. 8:17) (Ps. 59:16)
- You depend on God – He is your Source (Col. 3:4) (Ps. 119:147)
- You hear from God & He orders your day (Ps. 143:8)
- You are commanded to (Col. 4:2) (Lk. 18:1)
- You avoid distractions (Mk. 1:35)
- You give a firstfruits offering (Prov. 3:9-10) (Neh. 10:35-39)
- You don't have time not to. Give God the first part of your day, He will take care of the rest of yours (Mt. 6:33) miracle multiplication of your time, supernatural productivity, ideas, and strength
- You're better equipped to resist temptation (Mt. 26:41)

- You become what you focus on – you are what you think (Prov. 23:7)

I PUT MY TRUST IN GOD

*"But let all those rejoice who **put their trust in You**; let them ever shout for joy, because You defend them; let those also who love Your Name be joyful in You."* Psalm 5:11

Trusting God equals knowing God. Psalm 50:15 says, "I want you to trust Me in your times of trouble, so I can rescue you, and you can give Me glory."(TLB) We're all taught from childhood not to trust strangers. If I don't know God, how can I trust Him? One of God's Names is El Roi, God Who Sees. God knows every tear, every pang of guilt, every thought, every feeling of failure, disappointment, shame, every insecurity, and every fear you've ever experienced. He knows everything that has ever been done to you. Some of the other Names of God are Helper, Comforter, our Hope, our Strength, our Deliverer, our Guide, our Refuge, our Teacher, our Counselor, our Strong Fortress. You don't have to feel helpless or hopeless ever again. You don't have to depend on anyone else. You don't have to feel like the weight of the world is on your shoulders, wondering what you're going to do. When you're at your lowest point, when you've tried everything you know to do and still come up empty handed, that's actually when you're at your strongest, because God says, "I am at My strongest when you are at your weakest." (2 Cor. 12:10) When you have no other options *but* God and finally cry out to Him in desperation, He will show you that He really is who He says He is- the King of Glory, the Lord God Strong and Mighty, the Lord God Mighty In Battle. He does it so that you *know*, without any doubt, that it was *Him*, and you give Him *all* the credit. God is faithful. (Ps. 36:5) You are His child and He is the perfect Father. He wants to give you His best. *You can trust Him.*

THE LORD GOD DEFENDS ME

*"But let all those rejoice who put their trust in You; let them ever shout for joy, because **You defend them**; let those also who love Your Name be joyful in You." Psalm 5:11*

When I was in a coma, I was completely helpless. I had absolutely no knowledge of anything, much less control. I've been asked if I could hear or understand when people talked to me. I could not, but I came out of the coma with very vivid, very *real* memories of demons. It was so real, that I was tormented even after I was released from the hospital. I had to see a trauma specialist for PTSD. It seemed like the demons came every day, but I have no idea how often it actually happened. Each time they came, it was the same three. They would stand at the end of my bed and tell me lies about my pastor and the church I was in and people who are a part of the ministry. They would scream at me, "Just give in and it will all be over." But they never once touched me. I was strapped down, medicated, scared, unconscious. "Somehow" I prayed. Whether it was only in my mind, or out loud, I don't know. *I was in a coma.* Each time, the Holy Spirit inside me, the Spirit of the Living God, prayed the prayer that Jesus prayed in the garden the night before He was hung on the Cross. "Father, if it is Your will, take this cup away from me; nevertheless, Thy will be done." (Lk. 22:42) And then I would start thanking God for any and every thing I could think of. Every single time, the demons *ran*. They didn't just disappear, *they ran*. Then a man from the ministry I knew would stand at the end of my bed till my mind could rest. The man himself wasn't really in my room, but I figured it out later... I had nicknamed that man the Angel of the Lord because it seemed like he always showed up at the right time and took care of things he had no way of knowing needed fixing. In the Bible, the Angel of the Lord always says, "Fear not". Apparently, He looks scary. My body had already suffered enough that it caused a stroke. God was protecting me! After I came home, God revealed through Psalm 30 that He buried those demons in the grave that they had dug *for me*. That's how awesome God is! I give total praise to the Lord God, my Defender.

I LOVE GOD'S NAME

*"But let all those rejoice who put their trust in You; let them ever shout for joy, because You defend them; let **those also who love Your Name** be joyful in You." Psalm 5:11*

Although God's personal Name is Jehovah (Is. 42:8), He is called by many other names, which represent His nature, attributes, characteristics, everything that His Name implies and includes. It's who He is- His reputation, His Word, His authority, His glory. It's also who He is to *you*. Every name of God is available to you at all times. Spend some time looking into the Names of God and what they mean. Then think of ways in which these names are connected to you. For instance, Jehovah Rapha means the Lord our Healer. You can pray to Jehovah Rapha, (or Lord my Healer) and then just say the Name throughout your day. Say, "I praise You, Jehovah Rapha! Thank You, Lord for healing me, in the Name of Jesus!" You don't have to use the Hebrew name, though. Just say Jesus, Father God, or Holy Spirit. However *you* choose to say His Name in loving adoration, just say it. Remember, you are created in God's image, so who you are is vitally connected with who He is. The more you fall in love with who God is, the more you will see yourself as your Father God sees you and the more you will identify with Him and love yourself.

I AM JOYFUL IN THE LORD

*"But let all those rejoice who put their trust in You; let them ever shout for joy, because You defend them; let those also who love Your Name **be joyful in You.**" Psalm 5:11*

The joy of the Lord is your strength. (Neh. 8:10) It's what keeps you going when you think you're not going to make it another minute. Joy isn't just happiness. Happiness is temporary and depends on circumstances. Joy is a deep, inner awareness of God's goodness toward you.   It *isn't* the absence of trials, but the strength and assurance of God *with you* and *for you* in the midst of them, that defines joy. When you love God's Name, you depend on Him. He is ever faithful to love, deliver, defend, heal, restore, and meet you at your every point of need. Romans 12:12 tells us to rejoice in hope, be patient in times of trouble, and pray always. Hope brings great joy to someone without it. I can't begin to describe what a miserable person I was before I was born again. Even when I thought I was happy, I wasn't. I was simply owning my pain and wearing it like a badge of honor. God promises in Psalm 126:5, "Those who sow in tears shall reap in joy." Thank the Lord, I am now crowned with *His* joy and it has become a part of who I am and how I see myself. (Jn. 17:13) Since joy is a gift from the Holy Spirit, (Gal. 5:22-23) and His Spirit is alive inside of you, (1 Cor. 3:16) *you have joy*. You build it up by reading the Word, speaking the Word, and living according to the Word. Your joy will radiate for others to be drawn to the light of Christ, overflowing from *you*.

I AM MADE A LITTLE LOWER THAN THE ANGELS

*"For **You have made him a little lower than the angels**, and You have crowned him with glory and honor." Psalm 8:5*

In Genesis 1:26-27 it says that God created man in His own image and gave him dominion over all His creation on earth. Because of Adam's sin in the Garden of Eden, our image has become distorted and our dominion decreased, but Jesus humbled Himself and came to earth as a human being, to die for the redemption of every other living being's sins. When He rose from death, He defeated sin and death, once and for all. When Christ comes back, you will reign as royalty and judge the angels. Until then, you need to understand that there is absolutely nothing that has happened to you, that anyone says about you, or that you think about yourself, that will ever diminish God's incredible love for you, or His tender, elaborate, personal concern for every detail about you. You were created in love, in your Father's very own image, and Jesus lives inside of *you*, right now. Because you were created in God's image and only a *little* lower than the angels, there is no reason or right to think of yourself as anything less. You are God's masterpiece. (Eph. 2:10-NLT) You are fearfully and wonderfully made. (Ps. 139:14) You are the apple of God's eye! (Ps. 17:8) God has your name on the palm of His hand. (Is. 49:16) You were created with a purpose. (Jer. 29:11) If the all-knowing, all-powerful God of the whole universe thinks you're that special, then you most certainly are!

I AM CROWNED WITH GLORY

*"For You have made him a little lower than the angels, and **You have crowned him with glory** and honor." Psalm 8:5*

The Hebrew word for crowned in this verse means "encircled, compassed (for protection); adorned, honored". The Hebrew word for glory means "splendor, gloriousness". God surrounds you with His splendor and glory. You will find that when you are born again and have been spending time in the Word and in prayer, as you apply the Word and your life begins to change, people are drawn to you. There's just something *different*. You know what it is? It's Jesus! His light and His glory are alive, inside of *you*, and it naturally radiates from your very being. It's a beauty that can't be bought. It comes from *inside of you*, and pours forth. People who are in darkness instinctively move toward light. Daniel 12:3 says, "Those who are wise shall shine like the brightness of the firmament, and those who turn many to righteousness like the stars forever and ever." The glory that surrounds you brings others to know the source of that light, Jesus Christ. John 1:4 says, "In Him was life, and *the life was the light of men*." In John 8:12, Jesus says, "I am the light of the world. He who follows Me shall not walk in darkness, but have *the light of life*." Use your crown of glory to bring others into the light of righteousness, and your crown will shine like the stars forever.

I AM CROWNED WITH HONOR

*"For You have made him a little lower than the angels, and **You have crowned him with** glory and **honor."** Psalm 8:5*

You are crowned with honor by the King of Glory! A crown represents authority, beauty, majesty, and splendor. God gives you all that and more through Jesus Christ. I spent all my life believing I was "less than", a nobody that would never amount to anything. There were plenty of people telling me that and I believed it. Psalm 91:15 says, "He shall call upon Me, and I will answer him; I will be with him in trouble; I will deliver him *and* honor him." When I cried out to God to save me, He did. When I was in trouble, He rescued me, as many times as I needed Him to, even when I needed rescuing from myself. He delivered me from drugs, cigarettes, abuse, sickness, prison, death. But *honor me*? Why would He honor *me*? Because He honors His Word, and that's what His Word says. There are still people that don't recognize it and maybe never will, but there are also people that knew me before I surrendered to God that know without a doubt that He's done miracles in my life. I still feel unnoticed, underappreciated, misunderstood, by *people* sometimes, but I *know* that God is a Man of His Word, and His opinion is the only one that matters. I know what my life used to be like, and I have all the hope in the world for a better future, *because of God.*

Don't ever look at your circumstances and think you have to accept them. Don't agree with the devil. Whether people honor me or not, God does, and that honor will overflow eventually, for God's glory, not mine. I pray that by now you have started to see yourself as God sees you. It takes time, and it takes time for others to see you that way, too, especially if they aren't believers. When God honors you in front of them, though, be sure to thank Him and give Him all the credit. (Ps. 23:5)

I AM SHOWN THE PATH OF LIFE

"You show me the path of life; in Your presence is fullness of joy; at Your right hand are pleasures forevermore." Psalm 16:11

We're all on the path of life. The question is, which path, whose path, are you on? Has the path you've been following taken you where you thought you would be by now? If you could do it all over again, would you want a different path? A different life? If you still have breath in your body, it isn't too late to start over. God has a better way. Jesus says in John 14:6, "I am *the way, the truth, and the life.*" Jesus is the path to abundant life! (Jn. 10:10) Following Jesus isn't easy. There's a lot more to it than saying, "God bless you!" and sitting on the front pew every Sunday morning wearing a cool Christian t-shirt. It requires you to crucify your flesh, love the unlovable, and separate yourself from the world and its ways. It requires faith and endurance when all hell is breaking loose. It requires obedience and humility and total submission. Following Jesus requires you to read the Word and *do it*. Most people aren't willing to commit to that. They want to stay in their comfort zone, or they don't want to give up what *they* want. That's why Jesus said, "Narrow is the gate and difficult is the way which leads to life, and there are few who find it." (Mt. 7:14) You *have* found the way. Keep your eyes straight ahead and stay the course. When you put your

89

total trust in God and believe in His Son to lead you in all things, He will. "Your ears shall hear a word behind you, saying, "This is the way, walk in it," Whenever you turn to the right hand or whenever you turn to the left." (Is. 30:21) Deuteronomy 30:19-20 is titled The Blessing of Returning to God. It says, "I call Heaven and earth as witnesses today against you, that I have set before you life and death, blessing and cursing; therefore, choose life, that *both you and your descendants* may live; that you may love the Lord your God, that you may *cling to Him*, for *He is your life* and the length of your days." You are on the right path. Keep going. The best is yet to come.

I HAVE FULLNESS OF JOY IN GOD'S PRESENCE

*"You have shown me the path of life; **in Your presence is fullness of joy**; at Your right hand are pleasures forevermore."* Psalm 16:11

Fullness of joy is experiencing *all* the fullness of salvation, not just going to Heaven when you die. Did you know that eternal life begins as soon as you receive Christ as Lord of your life? Yep. The word "salvation" means delivered, rescued. Jesus rescued you from sin and its effects. He rescued you from the curse of the law by becoming a curse in your place. (Gal. 3:13) That means that you are free to live a changed life, a life free from sickness, poverty, bondage, fear, and oppression. Salvation includes not only forgiveness and eternal life, but also reconciliation, restoration, healing, peace, prosperity, adoption, sanctification. Any one of those things is reason enough for celebration, but you get the whole package, and so much more. You have the presence of God as your Friend, your Father, your Counselor, your Comforter, your Guide, your Helper, your Strength, your Refuge, at *all times*. His Spirit *lives inside of you*, so you're *always* in His presence. God doesn't intend for you to experience *some* salvation. He wants you to have it *all*. You are His beloved child and He wants you to live like it. Your fullness of joy is a testimony of His goodness in your life. It brings God glory when people see your life radically changed. It gives other

91

people hope for their own lives, and whether anybody wants to admit it or not, that's something that deep down inside, people long for. I did, but I didn't think there was enough hope to go around, not when it came to *me*. It wasn't till I saw what God had done in my cousin's life that I believed. She had been through a lot more than most people, and she lived pretty rough. She came to pick me up when I was getting out of jail once, and we just sat in the parking lot. I wanted to leave right away, but she pulled out her Bible and started talking to me about Jesus. Her eyes looked different. She wasn't talking crazy or yelling or cussing. She had a glow about her. She was happy! I thought, "If this is real, it's *got to be God!*" Looking back, I think about Jesus telling Andrew and Peter to follow Him and they immediately dropped their nets and went with Him. (Mt. 4:18-20) That's what I did that day with my cousin, because she finally had fullness of joy, and that gave me hope.

I AM THE APPLE OF GOD'S EYE

"Keep me as the apple of Your eye; hide me under the shadow of Your wings." Psalm 17:8

The only time I've ever heard the phrase "apple of my eye", was when my grandfather was breaking the news to me that he was about to die. I was 12 years old. He had been my mother and father, all in one, and he was very loving and good to me. His house was always my favorite place to go when things got too out of control at home. There were other places, but they weren't good. After I was born again, I could finally understand the Bible and remember what I had read, so I decided to read it cover to cover. That's when I came across Psalm 17:8. It jumped out at me. It still does. Every time I see it, I think, "God was talking to me even back then." So, what exactly does it mean? The word-for-word Hebrew translation literally means "little man of the eye". Have you ever seen your own reflection in someone else's eyes? First of all, you've got to be pretty close to that person, and they have to want you that close, or they would move away from you. It also means that that person was watching you closely. The meaning of the phrase "apple of my eye", as a whole, means something or someone that is cherished and adored above all else. This verse is David's prayer asking God for His protection against his enemies. Deuteronomy 32:10, The Song of Moses, says it this way, "He found him in a desert land, and in the waste howling wilderness; He led him about, He instructed him, He kept him as *the apple of His eye.*" That sounds like how God led me out of bondage. It tells me that all my life, all of *your life*, God has had His eye on all of you and me, to save us, to protect us, to teach us. You are intensely loved. You are treasured by Almighty God. You always have been and you always will be.

I AM HIDDEN UNDER THE SHADOW OF GOD'S WINGS

"Keep me as the apple of Your eye; **hide me under the shadow of Your wings."** *Psalm 17:8*

This is a reference to the way a mother hen gathers her children. In times past, the mother hen represented the embodiment of motherhood. A mother hen will fight anything that poses a threat to her babies, even animals that she herself is afraid of, while at the same time, pushing the chicks out of danger with her wings. While the chicks are small, she gathers them beneath her wings at night and sleeps the whole night with her wings covering the entire bunch. When the chicks are old enough, the mother hen flies up into a tree and watches over them while they develop their independence. Jesus says in Matthew 23:37, "O Jerusalem, Jerusalem...How often I wanted to gather your children together, as a hen gathers her chicks under her wings, but you were not willing!" God offers His love, provision, and protection to everyone, but not all the little chicks come running. Isaiah 30:15 says, "For thus says the Lord God, the Holy One of Israel: "In returning and rest you shall be saved; in quietness and confidence shall be your strength." But you would not." Small children often want to be independent, insisting, "I can do it myself!" They may try a thing to the point of frustration, or crying, when all they really needed was your help. It's the same for me and you. I ran away from God for so long. I didn't know that in submission and dependence, I could rest, knowing that when I can't, Father God can and does. Our help really does come from the Lord! (Ps. 121:2) That's in Scripture, but I didn't learn it there. I learned it by experiencing it for myself. You will, too. Psalm 91:1-4 says, "He who dwells in the secret place of the Most High, shall abide under the shadow of the Almighty. I will say of the Lord, He is my refuge and my fortress; my God, in Him I will trust. Surely He shall deliver you from the snare of the fowler and from the perilous pestilence. *He shall cover you with His feathers, and under His wings you shall take refuge*; His truth shall be your shield and buckler." The secret place is *in Him*. Jesus Christ is *the Word and Truth*. (Jn. 8:31-21) Rest in Him. Trust Him. You are hidden under His wings, safe and secure, in need of nothing, little chick.

I AM PROSPEROUS

*"Now **in my prosperity** I said, "I shall never be moved.""* Psalm 30:6

There's a lot of misunderstanding about prosperity, so I want you to know exactly what Biblical prosperity is. The Hebrew word for "prosperity" is "mot". It means security. Although I don't have a lot of money, all of my needs are met, beyond what is absolutely necessary. Every bit of that provision is by the hand of God. And even financially, I don't worry about where money will come from, because I know that *God* will supply all of my needs, according to *His riches* in glory, by Christ Jesus. (Php. 4:19) God multiplies the money that I do have, and makes it go way beyond what it's "supposed to". (2 Cor. 9:10-11) If you're just in it for the money aspect of prosperity, you're selling yourself way too short. "And God is able to make *all* grace *abound* toward *you*, that *you always*, having *all sufficiency* in *all things*, may have an *abundance* for *every* good work." (2 Cor. 9:8) God can most definitely make you financially rich, but a lot of people would then think they didn't need Him anymore. Matthew 6:33 tells us, "But seek *first* the Kingdom of God *and* His righteousness, and *all these things* shall be added to you." All what things? The blessings of the Lord. (Ps. 35:27) As a born again child of God, prosperity is part of your Divine inheritance. Strength and peace are your inheritance. (Ps. 29:11) The Hebrew word for peace is "shalom" - safety, well-being, happiness, healing, peace, wholeness, and yes, it includes economic provision as well. The essence of Biblical prosperity is living a blessed life. Why? Look back at 2 Corinthians 9:8, "For every good work." God gives you the power to get wealth *for the advancement of His Kingdom,* which includes charity to the less fortunate. A little further in 2 Corinthians 9:10-12, it says, "Now may He who supplies seed to the sower, and bread for food, supply and multiply the seed *you* have sown and increase the fruits of *your* righteousness, while *you* are enriched in *everything* for *all* liberality, which causes *thanksgiving* through us to God. For the administration of this service not only *supplies the needs of the saints*, but also is *abounding* through *many thanksgivings to God.*" That's why it's more blessed to give than to receive. (Acts 20:35) Because you have to be blessed before you can be a blessing. That's really what it's all about.

I SHALL NEVER BE MOVED

*"Now in my prosperity I said, "**I shall never be moved.**""* Psalm *30:6*

In your security and well-being, you will *never* waver, slip, be fallen in decay, or be removed. That's an excellent Biblical confession, but I want you to understand the context and implications of this verse, because I want you to live it out correctly. This psalm was written after David had taken a census of the people of Israel. He attempted to glorify himself, and didn't acknowledge God as the source of his abundance. God loved David and blessed him tremendously. God took David from the sheep pen to the palace, crowning David king over God's own people. This is the same David that God called "a man after My own heart". (Acts 13:22) But David had the people numbered to prove his self-sufficiency and feed his egotistical pride. God wasn't pleased, so He "hid His face" from David. In other words, He withdrew His favor. It is critically important to *always* remember that every good and perfect gift comes from God. (Jms. 1:17) Without God, you wouldn't have woke up this morning or even had a morning to wake up to. God is the God and Creator of *everything*. The known universe consists of planets, time, light, more than 2 trillion galaxies, each one having billions of stars, which God calls by name *individually*. (Ps. 147:4) And that's just what man knows about. The unobservable universe is so expansive that even a rough estimation is impossible. The same God that created all that with the words of His mouth delights in every last detail of your life. He knew you before He formed you in your mother's womb. (Jer. 1:5) He counts the number of hairs on your head. (Lk. 12:7) He wrote your name on the palm of His hand. (Is. 49:16) He delights in your prosperity. (Ps. 35:27, 3 Jn. 2) By yourself, you can only do so much. There are limits. But with God *ALL* things are possible. (Mt. 19:26) So, let's give God the glory by confessing, "In *God's* security and well-being, I will never waver, slip, be fallen in decay, or be removed, in the Name of Jesus. Amen!"

THE LORD HAS MERCY ON ME

*"Hear, O Lord, and **have mercy on me**; Lord, be my Helper!"*
Psalm 30:10

The Hebrew word for mercy means "to bend or stoop in kindness to an inferior". Asking God for mercy is a prayer asking for forgiveness, seen often throughout the psalms. Psalm 85:10 says, "Mercy and truth have met together, righteousness and peace have kissed." The word "mercy" expresses God's unwavering, uncompromising loyalty. "Truth" refers to our obedience and faithfulness to God's will and His Word. Through the Lord's mercies, we are not consumed. His compassions are new every morning. (Lam. 3:22-23) Jesus responded to an accusation that He was hanging out with the wrong crowd by saying, "I desire mercy and not sacrifice. For I did not come to call the righteous, but sinners, to repentance." (Mt. 9:13) This is a beautiful example of Jesus bending down and offering love, forgiveness, and compassion to the unworthy, undeserving outcasts, which if the truth be told, is all of us. "For we ourselves were also once foolish, disobedient, deceived, serving various lusts and pleasures, living in malice and envy, hateful and hating one another. But when the kindness and the love of God our Savior toward man appeared, not by works of righteousness which we have done, but *according to His mercy* He saved us, through the washing of regeneration and renewing of the Holy Spirit, whom He poured out on us abundantly through Jesus Christ our Savior." (Titus 3:3-6) Matthew 18:21-35 is the story of a servant to the king that owed the king a lot of money. The king had compassion on him and excused the debt, but then the man went to someone that owed him money and had the person put into prison. Matthew 5:7 says, "Blessed are the merciful, for *they shall obtain mercy*." And in Luke 6:36, "Therefore, be merciful, just as your Father also is merciful." You are your Father's dearly beloved child, therefore, be merciful just as your Father has been merciful to you.

THE LORD IS MY HELPER

"Hear, O Lord, and have mercy on me; **Lord, be my Helper!"**
Psalm 30:10

Do you see yourself as helpless? Not just that things are out of your control, but do you feel like you have no power to change anything because of who you are? I have some good news for you. Who you are is a child of the true living God. You have direct access to His throne, through Jesus. Prayer is the most powerful thing you can do to affect any situation. Psalm 22:4 says, "They trusted, and You delivered them." God fights for you. (Ex. 13:4) God protects you. (Deut. 33:29) He is Almighty God. (2 Chron. 14:11) The Lord is your Shepherd, your Provider, the Restorer of your soul, your Comforter. (Ps. 23) God turns your sadness into dancing. (Ps. 30:11) God answers your prayers. (Ps. 34:4) God upholds your life. (Ps. 54:4) He sustains you. (Ps. 55:22) God watches over you while you sleep. (Prov. 3:24) You can fully trust God. (Prov. 3:5-6) God takes you by the hand and leads you in the way you should go. (Is. 41:13) God is your Waymaker. (Is. 43:19) God gives you power and strength. (Is. 40:29) Before you were even born, God planned your life out with thoughts of peace and hope. (Jer. 1:5, 29:11) God takes away your worries. (Mt. 6:25) **Jesus died for your sins and gives you eternal life. (Jn. 3:16)** Jesus calls you His friend. (Jn. 15:13)

Jesus sent His Spirit to live inside you. (Jn. 16:7) God adopted you. (Rom. 8:15) God turns your messes into messages. (Rom. 8:28) God gives you hope by the power of the Holy Spirit. (Rom. 15:13) God makes a way of escape for you. (1 Cor. 10:13) God gives you His grace. (2 Cor. 12:9) God hears your prayers. (Php. 4:6) God gives you -the ability to do things that you can't do on your own. (Php. 4:13) God sanctifies you. (1 Thes. 5:23) God shields you from the devil's attacks. (2 Thes. 3:3) God gave you life. (1 Tim. 6:13) God is faithful. (2 Tim. 2:13) God gave you His Word. (Heb. 4:12) God gave you faith to overcome anything and everything. (Heb. 11) God has made you an heir to His Kingdom. (Jms. 2:5) God understands when you make mistakes. (Jms. 3:2) God gives you indescribable joy. (1 Ptr. 1:8) Jesus paid for your healing (1 Ptr. 2:24) God has given you *all* things that pertain to life and godliness. (2 Ptr. 1:3) God anointed you. (1 Jn. 2:20) Jesus loves you and gave His life for you. (1 Jn. 3:16) God made you His child. (1 Jn. 5:1) God keeps you from stumbling. (Jude 1:24) Jesus defeated Satan for *you*. (Rev. 12:11) You are *never* helpless. The Lord God is your Helper.

I COMMIT MY SPIRIT INTO GOD'S HAND

"Into Your hand I commit my spirit; You have redeemed me, O Lord God of truth." Psalm 31:5

This is actually a prayer of David, which Jesus also prayed on the Cross. (Lk. 23:46) Many people write affirmations on sticky notes or index cards and put them in places where they will see them often. Instead of affirmations, I believe in Scriptural confession. The Word of God does not return to Him without doing what it's sent out to do. (Is. 55:11) "For with the heart one believes unto righteousness, and with the mouth confession is made unto salvation." (Rom. 10:10) "But the Word is very near you, in your mouth and in your heart, that you may do it." (Deut. 30:14) I want to encourage you to use this prayer as your own confession, and to write it on something and speak it often. You can personalize it – "Lord, I commit (my life, my family, my health, the work of my hands, my ministry, my finances, my time, my service, my thoughts, my heart, my strength, my peace, etc.) into Your hand, in the Name of Jesus." The Hebrew word for hand in this verse means "open hand, indicating power, means, direction". Psalm 104:28 says, "You open Your hand, they are filled with good." One of the meanings of the word "commit" here means "to make overseer". You are trusting God to take complete control. Therefore, you are letting go of all control, all rights to control, over whatever you commit to Him. When I finally got up the courage and determination to leave my abusive boyfriend, I had to give that situation over to God. Every time I thought about him, I would say, "Oops, God! Sorry. That's yours. Take it back." And I kept speaking, "Lord, I commit my life into Your hand, in the Name of Jesus." Your life is in the hands of Almighty God, too. *All of it.*

I AM REDEEMED

"Into Your hand I commit my spirit; **You have redeemed me,** *O Lord God of truth." Psalm 31:5*

Redeemed means rescued. God has rescued me from abuse, neglect, addiction, homelessness, disease, illness, death, abandonment, joblessness, obesity, depression, mental illness, PTSD, loneliness, rejection, violence, poverty, torment, shame, sexual sin, low self esteem, crippling fear and shyness, betrayal, prison. Does any of this sound familiar? I used to ask God, "Why me, God?" but I realize now that God used those things to equip me to reach out to others, so that there would be nothing that I couldn't relate to when someone else felt like no one could ever understand them or be trusted to guide them. Had it not been for God's protection and deliverance, I would've never made it on my own. Genesis 50:20-21 says, "But as for me, you meant evil against me; *but God meant it for good,* in order to bring it about as it is this day, *to save many people alive.* Now therefore, do not be afraid; I will provide for you *and* your little ones. *And he comforted them and spoke kindly to them."* Your pain has a purpose. The thing that caused it was sent to destroy you, but Jesus paid for your redemption through His suffering, death, and resurrection. If you were stranded in the ocean and a helicopter lowered a rope to you, you would have to reach out and grab that rope to be rescued, right? In the same way, you have to receive what Jesus offers you. When you do, you use what Christ did for you to rescue someone else, by comforting them, speaking kindly to them, and *pointing them to what Jesus did for you.* That's why you were born with a target on your forehead, because the devil only attacks what's valuable, and you are a mighty warrior for the Kingdom of God on the face of this earth. You were redeemed to save many people alive, as it is this day.

MY TIMES ARE IN GOD'S HAND

*"**My times are in Your hand**; deliver me from the hand of my enemies, and from those who persecute me." Psalm 31:15*

Notice that verse doesn't say "if I have enemies" or "if I'm persecuted". Whether your enemies and persecutors are seen or unseen, you have them. David did, too. Rather than worrying, David prayed and trusted God with the outcome. When you pray "My times are in Your hand" it's the same as praying "My life is in Your hand" or "My future is in Your hand" or "My family is in Your hand". Prayer is submissive dependence on God for everything. Everything. Everything. Think of how a baby is dependent on its mother for everything. That baby's times are in its mother's hand, at least while it's still a baby. The baby is dependent on its mother to take care of every one of its needs. Proverbs 19:21 (NLT) says, "You can make many plans, but the Lord's purpose will prevail." God is in complete control. Sometimes you have to go through things that look like you're not going to make it, but if your trust is in God, He will use that situation for His purpose, His glory, and your growth and highest good. Maybe you've heard it referred to more commonly as a blessing in disguise. Every person used mightily of God began with circumstances that could have devastated their lives. Jesus, David, Paul, Joseph, Ruth, Esther, Daniel, Moses. All of them faced circumstances that would have made most people give up. The thing that made them different is that each one of those people chose to rely fully on God, so God not only blessed them, but many others were blessed by their obedience. Anytime you give something over to God, big or small, it then becomes His. Sometimes He will direct you to act on certain things, other times He wants you to "be still and know that He is God." (Ps. 46:10) Either way, it's God's to deal with and not yours, so you really don't have to worry about it. Just believe and do not doubt and whatever you have asked in prayer, *believing*, you will receive. (Mt. 21:21-22)

I AM DELIVERED FROM MY ENEMIES AND THOSE WHO PERSECUTE ME

"My times are in Your hand; **deliver me from the hand of my enemies, and from those who persecute me."** *Psalm 31:15*

Persecution is defined as "hostility or ill treatment, especially because of race or political or religious beliefs". It is also defined as "persistent annoyance or harassment". Christians certainly face persecution from the world, but even among other Christians, persecution is pretty common. How? Gossip, backbiting, criticism, judgment, legalism, manipulation, selfish ambition, jealousy. Yes, even in the church. Those same people try to convince you that God co-signs their behavior. He doesn't. I call them the Pharisees or the religion police. They are the reason a lot of people "aren't into religion", because they've had bad experiences in the church and never went back. The enemy isn't the person persecuting you, it's an evil spirit working through them, but it still feels the same to the person being targeted. Persecution will come, no doubt. The Bible says "when" it comes, not "if". (Mt. 5:11) In Matthew 5:12 it says, "Rejoice and be exceedingly glad, for great is your reward in Heaven, for so they persecuted the prophets before you." Not only that, it's a sign that you have a major breakthrough heading your way. If you respond according to God's Word, in love, (Mt. 5:44) it will keep you from re-taking that test over and over. Your breakthrough is imminent. Another reason to rejoice is that you were counted worthy of persecution, meaning that you were identified by the enemy as "one of them". In Acts 5:41, the apostles were beaten and released from prison, but it says that they left "rejoicing that they were counted worthy to suffer shame for His Name." Remember, the devil only attacks what is a threat to him and valuable to God. God has delivered you more times than you will ever know, even before you were a Christian. He is still in the rescue business. Especially now that you're "one of them".

I AM PROTECTED

"You are my hiding place; You shall preserve me from trouble; You shall surround me with songs of deliverance." Psalm 32:7

One of the definitions for the Hebrew word that translates as "hiding place" is "secret place". Psalm 91 is titled "Safety of Abiding in the Presence of God". Verses 1-2 say, "He who dwells in the secret place of the Most High shall abide under the shadow of the Almighty. I will say of the Lord, "He is my refuge and my fortress; my God, in Him I will trust."" I can't begin to tell you how many times I've ran to God, sometimes with absolutely no words, just tears, and sat in His presence or poured over His Word, seeking comfort and safety. God provided that for me out of His grace and mercy. He will do the same for you, too. You don't have to understand it. Just believe it. Notice in Psalm 91, it says, "He who *dwells"*. That means "He who *lives in, stays in, remains in"*. To live in the secret place of the Most High, you have to stay in God's presence, not just when you want something. The word "abide" means to remain stable in, to conform to, and to accept or act in accordance with. That means that you have to continue in the Word, in prayer, in applying the Truth to your life, day after day, moment by moment. You have to do it intentionally, do it tired, do it afraid, do it when it hurts, do it when it doesn't make sense, do it when it's hard, do it when it isn't what you want to do, do it when it goes against what you've always believed or what anyone says or thinks. Do it *trusting God*, believing that He is who He says He is, that He will do what He says He will do, and that you are His beloved child and there is no safer place than in the hands of your Father.

I AM SURROUNDED WITH SONGS OF DELIVERANCE

"You are my hiding place; You shall preserve me from trouble; **You shall surround me with songs of deliverance.**" Psalm 32:7

I've shared with you a lot of the things the Lord has delivered me from. He continues to deliver me, even now. Deliverance is part of salvation. It's being rescued from sin, sickness, eternal death, spiritual oppression and bondage, spiritual death, spiritual attack, and everyday difficulties. A couple of years ago, I stopped listening to secular music. The kind of secular music I usually listened to didn't glorify God or edify me. It was very destructive and negative. I started listening to Christian music, even if it wasn't the "type" music I was used to. I wasn't listening to enjoy it, so much as I was listening to glorify God. Two years ago, I started hearing worship music in my sleep. I was doing a lot of service in the ministry, really seeking God through serving God and the people that He had called me to care for. For the first time in my life, I fell asleep every night as soon as my head hit the pillow. I had dreams, but in the dreams, I could hear worship music. I would wake up with songs in my head. I've listened to music my whole life, but I've never heard music in my sleep until I started hearing the worship songs. A year later, God delivered me from death, from an illness that by itself, most people don't live through. Additionally, I had a brain infection and I suffered a stroke from the stress on my body. I think of Daniel, whose prayer was heard by God as soon as he prayed, but the angel Michael was at war for 21 days, to get that prayer delivered. It took 2 months, but I was delivered. In that 2 months, God sang over me with songs of deliverance. I know He did, because *I'm alive.* There is *nothing* that shows *any* sign that *anything* ever happened, except a couple of tiny scars. One of my favorite Scriptures is Zephaniah 3:17. "The Lord your God in your midst, the Mighty One, will save; He will rejoice over you with gladness, He will quiet you with His love, He will rejoice over you with singing". Before you even took your first breath, God was singing over you. He's sang over you your whole life. He sings over you now. Tune in and listen for His song.

I AM SINGING GOD A NEW SONG

"Sing to Him a new song; play skillfully with a shout of joy."
Psalm 33:3

I told you how, a couple of years ago, I made a conscious decision to stop listening to secular music and listen only to Christian music, even if I didn't particularly like it so much. Proverbs 18:21 says, "Death and life are in the power of the tongue, and those who love it will eat its fruit." When I think back on all the rotten fruit I ate, singing songs that were derogatory and celebratory of everything that represents darkness, singing over myself, people around me, my circumstances, the world itself, it's shocking. You get what you say, so be careful what you're singing to. Ezekiel 28 describes Satan as an angel that had musical instruments prepared specifically for him the day he was created. Satan fell from Heaven as a result of his pride. He wanted to be like God. In the first verses of Ezekiel 28, Satan is described as "full of wisdom and perfect in beauty". He was *attractive*. There's a lot of music in our culture that *sounds* good. But think about some of the words that you've spoken while singing to that music. I'm not saying that all secular music is from Satan, but he sure found a slick way of promoting his kingdom in music that glorifies sex, drugs, violence, and even hell itself. Satan's agenda is to kill, steal, and destroy. (Jn. 10:10) He is a liar and the father of all lies. (Jn. 8:44) Jesus came to give you abundant life. (Jn. 10:10) God created music for *His* glory. (Job 38:7) Christians are called to honor God in all that they do and with all that they have and all that they are. Music is a part of that. I have learned that, no matter what kind of music you like, there is Christian music in that genre that glorifies God. Rap, metal, country, blues, jazz, R&B, classical, you name it, there's worship music. (I haven't heard any disco...) You serve the Lord, who gave you abundant, new life through His Son, Jesus. Sing Him a new song!

I BLESS THE LORD AT ALL TIMES

"I will bless the Lord at all times; His praise shall continually be in my mouth." Psalm 34:1

Worship and thanksgiving are our responses to God's mercy, His goodness, His God-ness. Even when things are falling apart, when the whole world is coming against you, when it looks like things just couldn't get any worse, bless the Lord. You do have choices. You can cry or stand still in fear or lash out in anger or plot and scheme or call your mother. Or you can thank God anyway. You can worship Him anyway. In the middle of the storm, you can sing praises to the One who makes the winds and waves obey Him. (Mt. 8:24-27) 2 Samuel 22:4 says, "I call upon *the Lord, who is worthy to be praised*, and I am saved from my enemies." The Lord is great, and greatly to be praised. (Ps. 96:4) Bless the Lord in the sunshine and the rain, the good times and the bad. How is that even possible? You get to know Him. *Really* know Him, by spending time with Him, learning from Him, talking to Him, seeking Him with all your heart. To bless the Lord is to praise Him, to *magnify Him*. What does a magnifying glass do? It makes something bigger. It allows you to get a better focus on what you're trying to see, while making everything else smaller in comparison. In other words, shift your focus onto God, away from your circumstances. When Peter stepped out of the boat in Matthew 14:29-30, he walked on water with Jesus. It wasn't until he took his eyes off Jesus and looked at his circumstances that he began to sink. The Bible says he was overcome by fear. Jesus rescued Peter anyway, but He asked him why he doubted. When fear and doubt try to overtake you, look to Jesus. Follow Jesus. Stand on the Word. Read it, speak it, think on it, and bless the Lord! You *are* a water walker, too!

THE LORD'S PRAISE IS CONTINUALLY IN MY MOUTH

*"I will bless the Lord at all times; **His praise shall continually be in my mouth.**" Psalm 34:1*

"Oh clap your hands, all you peoples! Shout to God with the voice of triumph! For the Lord Most High is awesome; He is a great King over all the earth." (Ps. 47:1-2) "Blessing and glory and wisdom, thanksgiving and honor and power and might, be to our God forever and ever." (Rev. 7:12) "The Lord is my strength and song, and He has become my salvation; He is my God, and I will praise Him." (Ex. 15:2) "Therefore I will give thanks to You, O Lord, among the Gentiles, and sing praises to Your Name." (1 Sam. 22:50) "Now therefore, our God, we thank you and praise Your glorious Name." (1 Chron. 29:13) "I will praise the Lord according to His righteousness, and will sing praise to the Name of the Lord Most High." (Ps. 7:17) "I will praise You, O Lord, with my whole heart; I will tell of all Your marvelous works." (Ps. 9:1) "I will be glad and rejoice in You; I will sing praise to Your Name, O Most High." (Ps. 9:2) "Be exalted, O Lord, in Your own strength! We will sing and praise Your power." (Ps. 21:13) "I will declare Your Name to My brethren; in the midst of the assembly I will praise You." (Ps. 22:22) "The Lord is my strength and my shield; my heart trusted in Him, and I am helped; therefore my heart greatly rejoices, and with my song I will praise Him." (Ps. 28:7) "Sing praise to the Lord, you saints of His, and give thanks at the remembrance of His holy Name." (Ps. 30:4) "And my tongue shall speak of Your righteousness and of Your praise all the day long." (Ps. 35:28) "Sing praises to God, sing praises! Sing praises to our King, sing praises!" (Ps. 47:6) "Great is the Lord, and greatly to be praised in the city of our God, in His holy mountain." (Ps. 48:1) "O Lord, open my lips, and my mouth shall show forth Your praise." (Ps. 51:5) "I will freely sacrifice to You; I will praise Your Name, O Lord, for it is good." (Ps. 54:6) "In God (I will praise His Word), In the Lord (I will praise His Word.)" (Ps. 56:10) "To You, O my Strength, I will sing praises; for God is my defense, my God of mercy." (Ps. 59:17) "Because Your lovingkindness is better than life, my lips shall praise You." (Ps. 63:3) "My mouth shall praise You with joyful lips." (Ps. 63:5) "Sing out the honor of His Name; make His praise glorious." (Ps. 66:2) "Oh, bless our God, you peoples! And make the voice of His praise to be heard." (Ps. 66:8) "I will praise the Name of God with a song, and I will magnify Him with thanksgiving." (Ps. 69:30)

THE ANGEL OF THE LORD ENCAMPS ALL AROUND ME

"The Angel of the Lord encamps all around those who fear Him, and delivers them." Psalm 34:7

Twice in my life, I believe, I have seen the Angel of the Lord. I've told you about one of those times, when I was in a coma. The first time, though, I was sitting in a cheap motel room where there had been 5 murders in 3 weeks. I had been awake longer than that, but had only recently moved into the motel. My brother had been killed a month or so earlier. I was doing the best I could to kill the pain, but I ran out of drugs. I sat on the edge of the bed with the door open, waiting for my dealer's truck to pull up. I was awakened by the housekeeper, telling me, "Baby, I know you feel comfortable, but there's a lot of bad people around here. You need to keep your door closed if you're going to lay down." I had accidentally fallen asleep. I was clearly and immediately aware of talking to my brother. In fact, it was more real to me than talking to the housekeeper. I had dreamed that I was still sitting on the edge of the bed and my brother was standing in the doorway, blocking the entire doorway with his body. He was huge, muscular, dressed in Roman type armor, and he had large wings. His arms were folded across his chest. I kept trying to speak to him, but he wouldn't talk to me. For a long time, I thought it was my brother, there to protect me, but after the similar experience I had when I was in a coma, I believe now that it was the Angel of the Lord, encamped around me, presenting Himself in an image that I could bear. In Genesis 22:11, Abraham is about to sacrifice his son Isaac, and the Angel of the Lord tells him to stop. In verse 12, the wording reveals that the Angel of the Lord is God. This is also revealed in verses 15 and 16. The fear of Lord is the reverence and respect of the Lord, but it's also actual fear, the thing that keeps you from doing your own thing, especially when you *know* what God has to say about it. You are a God-fearing, Holy Ghost filled, faithful, obedient, Christ-following child of the Most High God, and you are Divinely protected by the Angel of the Lord!

THE ANGEL OF THE LORD DELIVERS ME

"The angel of the Lord encamps all around those who fear Him, and delivers them." Psalm 34:7

In Genesis 31:11, the Angel of the Lord is speaking to Jacob. In verse 13 He says, "I am the God of Bethel, where you anointed the pillar and where you made a vow to Me." Genesis 28:19-20 is where Jacob made a vow at Bethel *to God*. In Exodus 3:11, the Angel of the Lord appeared to Moses in a burning bush. When He spoke to Moses in verse 13, He said, "I am the God of your father, the God of Abraham, the God of Isaac, and the God of Jacob." He went on to instruct Moses on the deliverance of the Israelites from Egypt. In Exodus 14:19, it is the Angel of God who went before the people and who went behind them, *encamping them,* surrounding them on every side, protecting them. That's how the Angel of the Lord delivers you *still*. You may not see Him, but you can see His deliverance. You may not see the Red Sea, but it still parts for you to walk through, and it still swallows up your enemies, to God's glory! There is no way to comprehend the ways in which God works but by His grace and mercy they are the same yesterday, today, and forever. I have come to believe that the places and some of the people from the Bible are still very much alive- in the spiritual realm. I received this knowledge by revelation, but I actually received confirmation when I heard Bishop Eddie Long say, "Jerusalem isn't just a place, it's a *dimension*." The things that are unseen are *more real* because they are *spiritual* and they are *eternal*. It takes a Spiritual Deliverer to rescue you from those kinds of entities. It takes Almighty God.

I SEEK THE LORD

*"The young lions lack and suffer hunger; but **those who seek the Lord** shall not lack any good thing." Psalm 34:10*

My first thought on this was how God supplies our needs, even when everybody else is experiencing effects of a bad economy, sickness, etc. I did a word study on the original Hebrew words, and then sat back to think and pray. God gave me a new direction for this page. The Hebrew meaning for seek is "to seek or ask, specifically for worship- diligently inquire, question, require". When you seek after God in prayer and in His Word, when you rely on *Him*, rather than on yourself, your paycheck, someone else, when you dare to ask, dare to trust, dare to believe God and God alone, to answer prayers so big that there could be no other possibility *but God* for those prayers to be answered, it pleases Him. It's a way of saying that you believe that God is able to do exceedingly, abundantly above all that we ask or think. (Eph. 3:20) Matthew 6:33 says, "Seek first the Kingdom of God and His righteousness, and all these things shall be added to you." Don't get me wrong. I don't mean to seek God for what He will give you. I'm talking about seeking God passionately, with hunger in your heart. I used to be a waitress, and when business was slow, they would let one or two waitresses go home, since we worked mainly on tips. I would always volunteer to go early, even if it meant the possibility of not making money for that night, because I couldn't wait to get home and lay out in the floor and spend time with my Beloved. I looked for Him in my Bible, reading and listening for Him to speak to me. Sometimes I would play worship music and write out love letters (prayers). I intentionally went after Jesus, and did so with great expectation. Matthew 2 says when Christ was born, the wise men travelled from the east, following the star announcing His birth. They didn't sit around waiting for Jesus to grow up and find them. They didn't interrogate Mary and Joseph. They didn't ask to see the birth certificate. They didn't ask Mary and Joseph for a co-pay. They came seeking Jesus, the newborn Christ. The wise men came with gifts *for* Him, not asking for anything *from* Him, except to worship Him. You are wise in seeking Him, too.

I DO NOT LACK ANY GOOD THING

*"The young lions lack and suffer hunger; but those who seek the Lord **shall not lack any good thing.**" Psalm 34:10*

The Hebrew word for "good" here isn't just good, as we know it in English. The Hebrew word for "good" translates as "beautiful, best, better, bountiful, cheerful, at ease, favor, joyful, kindness, loving, merry, most pleasant, pleasure, precious, prosperity, sweet, wealth, welfare". Not only that, but this verse says that those who seek the Lord shall not lack *any* good thing. ANY. Every bit of that good belongs to *you* when you seek the Lord. The phrase "young lions" represents self-sufficiency. When you try to do things in your own ability, you are limited. When you fully depend on God, your sufficiency is supernatural. It's God's sufficiency. His resources and power and ability are unlimited. He is *the Source* of all power, might, and majesty. Every blessing available is in His hand alone. That doesn't mean that you get everything you want or expect, but your needs are met and you get overly and abundantly above that. You also get what's best for you, which sometimes means that you *don't* get what you want, but it's for your best interest. If you're a parent, you know exactly what I'm talking about. There's nothing wrong with giving a child a cookie, but that doesn't mean they can have cookies for breakfast, lunch, and dinner. You know better, so you have to make sure that they get nutritious food regularly, and a cookie every now and then. You want them to grow and be healthy. God wants the same for you. He wants you to be the best that you can be, to live the best life possible, and sometimes that means saying no. Instead, you will grow into a healthy, mature person that lives a fruitful, peaceful, joyous life. I used to have severe depression, panic and anxiety attacks, and migraine headaches several times a week. I was on medication for years. Nothing helped until God delivered me. I tried on my own to stop using drugs for over 40 years. Every attempt ended up with me sinking deeper into addiction than when I began my efforts to stop. I was consumed with guilt, shame, and failure. When I finally stopped trying and *fully trusted God and His Word* ("I will heal their backsliding. I will love them freely." Hosea 14:3) God took addiction from me completely. Seek God for God, but believe Him for all the fullness He has for *you*. It's His will for you.

I KEEP MY LIPS FROM SPEAKING DECEIT

"Keep your tongue from evil, and your lips from speaking deceit."
Psalm 34:13

Whoo! This was a tough one for me. I spoke so much evil I didn't even know it was coming out of my mouth. When it was called to my attention, I tried to catch myself. I was appalled at how nasty my mouth was. And I couldn't stop! I tried for about a week, but finally I got on my knees and said, "God, I can't do this! If you really want me to stop, help me. Do it *for me*. I can't." He heard me. I didn't speak any cuss words for a while, and when I did, I believe it was because I wasn't focused on God as much as I had been before. The Bible says that we are either justified or condemned by our words. (Mt. 12:37) Your words reflect what's in your heart. (Mt. 12:34) Speaking evil consists of all kinds of profanity, adversity, arguing, slander, gossip, complaining, grievous, hurtful, wicked speech. Deceit is lying, but did you know that speaking anything that doesn't line up with the Word of God is also deceit? That's right. God's Word is Truth, so to speak anything contrary to that Word is a lie. So is twisting the Word to pervert the Truth to one's own agenda. Everything you do is a message to others. What would you think of someone who claimed to be sold out for Christ, but was argumentative, prideful, selfish, who lied, stole, was promiscuous, who drank excessively? There are people that do that, offering the excuse that we are forgiven, or "there is no condemnation". That's true, but we are also called to be a light to others. (Mt. 5:14-16). All those things are of the flesh. Romans 8:7-8 says that the carnal mind is active opposition or hostility against God, and those who are in the flesh *cannot* please God. The answer to pleasing God and controlling the works of the flesh is found in Galatians 5:16-17- "I say then: walk in the Spirit, and you shall not fulfill the lusts of the flesh. For the flesh lusts against the Spirit, and the Spirit against the flesh; and these are contrary to one another, so that you do not do the things you wish." Even Paul had struggles with the flesh. (Rom. 7:15-20). It's a process, one that you have to be conscious of daily. Ask the Holy Spirit to reveal any ways in which you sin by the words you speak, and then make the choice to correct that, so that you will be pleasing to God and a pure light for others to follow.

I DEPART FROM EVIL AND DO GOOD

"Depart from evil and do good; seek peace and pursue it." Psalm
34:14

The definition I found online for the word 'depart' is "leave,
especially in order to start a journey". Imagine that you were in a
place where every form of evil was present, every form of sickness,
violence, sadness, hatred, suffering, corruption, poverty, abuse,
slavery. Now imagine that someone came to rescue you and take you
to a place where you were completely safe and completely cared for.
A place where you were loved without limits, based on the heart of
the one who rescued you. Wouldn't your response to that person's
goodness toward you be to do everything you could to show them
how grateful you are and to adopt their way of living and believing
so that you could remain there? You may even desire to help them
bring others out of the same place that you had been rescued from.
Your journey began when you were born again. You were delivered
from sin and sickness and death. Your life in Christ begins with the
death of your old life and the birth of your new life in Christ. (Gal.
2:20) God can and does deliver instantly, but because you still live in
the flesh, you have to intentionally strive toward godliness. This is
the part of the journey where transformation takes place. God uses
your journey to build *His* character in you, so that your life can be

used for the benefit of others. God is including *you* in the process of rescuing people that are still in that place of fear, torment, shame, worthlessness, anger, jealousy, whatever that place may be. The same place that you were rescued from is still full of people desperate to get out, with no hope that a way of escape is even possible. God can use you just like He used Moses to lead His people out of captivity, oppression, and bondage. Your journey is the reason for someone else to believe that there is a way out. That's why it's so vitally important that you crucify the flesh, because *you* are the visible evidence of Christ's saving grace.

I SEEK PEACE AND PURSUE IT

*"Depart from evil and do good; **seek peace and pursue it.**" Psalm 34:14*

I've seen t-shirts that say, "Know God, know peace. No God, no peace." The word peace usually means "lack of conflict" or "a state of tranquility". In this verse, the word peace comes from the Hebrew word *shalom*. Shalom is so much more than 'peace', as we know in English. In the Bible, shalom is a part of God's covenant with His people. (Ez. 37:26) It is a state of overall wellbeing, completeness, good health, long life, tranquility, prosperity, safety, security, blessing, joy. It is both physical and spiritual. One translation is "nothing missing, nothing broken". Another is "to live well". One of the Names of God is Jehovah Shalom – The Lord is Peace. (Jdgs. 6:24) Shalom isn't necessarily the absence of problems in your life, but rather your response to them. You no longer have to worry about things because you're covered by Almighty God, and He's all powerful and faithful. It's His business to handle everything that concerns you. Like joy, shalom doesn't depend on circumstances. Shalom is a peace that passes all understanding. (Php. 4:7) When Christ was born, the angels announced shalom on earth. (Lk. 2:14) This peace, total and complete, is possible only through Christ, the Prince of Peace. (Is. 9:6) When you set your focus on God, commit your heart and your life to Him, and trust in Him, you enter into the covenant that promises perfect shalom. The pursuit of peace is your responsibility, and it should be sought after aggressively. It's rest for your soul. The best way I know to seek peace and pursue it is to seek *God* and pursue *Him*. "But seek first the Kingdom of God *and* His righteousness, and all these things shall be added to you." (Mt. 6:33) "Be anxious for nothing, but in everything, by prayer and supplication, with thanksgiving, let your requests be made known to God, and *the peace of God, which surpasses all understanding*, will guard your hearts and minds through Christ Jesus." (Php. 4:6-7) Instead of focusing on life and its demands, focus on the One who gave you life. You will have unshakable, unwavering confidence and you can rest in His ability. "You will keep him in perfect peace, whose mind is stayed on You, because He trusts in You." (Is. 26:3)

THE EYES OF THE LORD ARE ON ME

"The eyes of the Lord are on the righteous, and His ears are open to their cry." Psalm 34:15

2 Chronicles 16:9 says, "For the eyes of the Lord run to and fro throughout the whole earth, to show Himself strong on behalf of those whose heart is loyal to Him." The eyes of the Lord are all-seeing, all-knowing, everywhere at all times. Yet, as all-powerful as they are, they are tender, loving, protective, meticulous in watching over His children. "Behold, the eye of the Lord is on those who fear Him, on those who hope in His mercy." (Ps. 33:18) "And there is no creature hidden from His sight, but all things are naked and open to the eyes of Him to whom we must give account." (Heb. 4:13) "For he who touches you touches the apple of His eye." (Zech. 2:8) God knows everything that has ever been done to you to hurt you, offend you, embarrass you. He knows everything you've ever had to do that made you feel like anything less than the person He created you to be. And He loves you. Don't think that because you went through something that it was God that caused it. This may not be the case for everyone, but I know it's the case for a lot of people, so I'm addressing it. I've told you, I used to ask God, "Why me?" Especially if He knew the things that were happening to me. Why did He let it happen? Today, I know that God carried me through

those things, to help others find healing that may not find it otherwise, and to point them to Him as the Healer. God sees it all, and you better believe that no injustice goes unpunished. You may not see it happen, but God does. "Understand, therefore, that the Lord your God is indeed God. He is the faithful God who keeps His covenant for a thousand generations and constantly loves those who love Him and obey His commands. But He does not hesitate to punish and destroy those who hate Him." (Deut. 7:9-10) You are God's precious child. As much as you love anybody on this earth, you can't begin to imagine how much you are loved by your Heavenly Father. To hurt you hurts Him. Not only does He watch over you, He has guided you throughout your entire life. "I will instruct you and teach you in the way you should go; I will guide you with My eye." (Ps. 32:8) Even in the worst things you've ever been through, it could have been worse. Have you ever thought about it that way? You aren't alone. You are dearly loved and under Divine protection.

I AM RIGHTEOUS

*"The eyes of the Lord are on **the righteous**, and His ears are open to their cry." Psalm 34:15*

By all outward appearances, there is no righteousness in me whatsoever. My past screams unrighteousness, but by the grace and mercy of God, I can confidently proclaim that I AM RIGHTEOUS. I am made righteous through Christ, and *His righteousness.* (Rom. 3:21-26) "For He made Him who knew no sin to be sin for us, that we might become the righteousness of God in Him." (2 Cor. 5:21) There is absolutely no one who lives a perfect and sinless life. Jesus was the only one ever to do that. Praise God, that every sin, every mistake, every dirty deed ever done is covered by the Blood of Jesus. It not only cancels our sin, it erases it from God's memory altogether. (Heb. 8:12) That doesn't mean you can keep on doing things that are wrong and it goes unnoticed. (Rom. 6:1-2) It means that your consciousness is tuned to righteousness and the Holy Spirit will convict you of anything that needs to be forgiven. You will be more mindful of things than before and you will have a desire to do good, to please God, and to live according to His righteousness. Another big part of righteousness is believing God. It isn't just about *doing* right, it's also about *believing* right, believing what God says in His Word. Romans 4 tells about Abraham, who lied about Sarah being his wife, as *believing God* and it was accounted to him for righteousness. David, who was an adulterer and a murderer, also had *his faith* accounted to him as righteousness. When you willfully turn from wrong to right and *believe* that God has forgiven you, and you follow His ways and *believe His Word*, you are made righteous through the Blood of Jesus. There are no ifs, ands, or buts about it. It doesn't matter what you've done. Christ took it from you. It may not feel like it, but feelings don't matter. They don't! YOU ARE RIGHTEOUS. God says so! That's how faith works - believing no matter what it looks like, *what it feels like*, what anybody says or thinks, trusting God, believing God, standing on the Word of God, over and over and over.

THE LORD'S EARS ARE OPEN TO MY CRY

*"The eyes of the Lord are on the righteous, and **His ears are open to their cry."** Psalm 34:15*

God is ever watchful, all-knowing, even toward the secret things of the heart. When you appear to be okay to the people around you, but inside you're holding on to pain or anger, holding back tears of despair or feelings of unworthiness, or whatever you're keeping hidden behind a smile, *God knows*. And He cares. He loves you. Really loves you, with a love you can't even begin to imagine. You are the delight of His heart, *the apple of His eye*. When you think there's no one that will understand, no one that can help you, no one who thinks you're important enough to listen to, you might be right. Except for God. Even if there is someone who can help you, they can't do what God can do for you. And they can't completely understand because they're not you, but the Spirit of God is in you. He does understand. When Christ took the form of a man, He experienced life as we know it, not just from a Divine perspective. Whatever you are hanging onto, *God already knows*. If your child had a bomb in their pocket and thought that you would be mad at them, wouldn't you rather that child give you the bomb, than letting it explode in their pocket? Of course you would. And you wouldn't be angry or indifferent toward the situation. God doesn't watch over you to punish you or because He doesn't have anything better to do. He watches over you as the best loving, protective Father there is. He wants only good for you. "For I know the thoughts that I think toward you, says the Lord, thoughts of peace and not of evil, to give you a future and a hope." (Jer. 29:11) Prayer is powerful, but I can honestly tell you that the prayers where I've literally cried out to God in desperation, not trying to say the right thing or think of what to say or follow any pattern, just pouring the contents of my broken heart out, spilling them all over Daddy God's shoulder, He has answered powerfully and immediately. God hears the very breath you breathe. Trust Him with your heart. Cry out to Him. He's listening.

I AM JOYFUL IN THE LORD

*"And **my soul shall be joyful in the Lord**; it shall rejoice in His salvation." Psalm 35:9*

Your joy is a big deal to God, so it should be a big deal to you, too. Joy isn't the same as happiness. Happiness depends on circumstances. Joy is full in spite of them. It's a deep inner satisfaction that comes from abiding in God because you know He's in control and you trust that no matter what's going on, God's got you, and He's working everything out for your good and His glory. That kind of joy remains, even when everything is in total chaos and it looks like the world is about to come crashing down around you. You can keep your joy by trusting God. This does an amazing thing. It serves as a weapon against the devil and all his ways. See, he tries to get you to live off your feelings, in reaction to the mess he likes to throw around. If you get all upset and bent out of shape over every little thing, you might just completely unhinge over some big stuff. That's exactly what the devil wants you to do. You can stop him dead in his tracks by responding with joy. Have you ever met people that just like to push your buttons? They don't need a reason, there doesn't have to be a point to it, they just enjoy your emotional meltdown? What would happen if you responded with a sweet, sincere smile? Maybe even surprised them with a coffee or flowers?

Or you sang to yourself, "Jesus, you're all I need." Not in a sarcastic or self-righteous kind of way, but from your heart. The joy of the Lord will always win because darkness can't remain in light. (Jn. 1:5) Joy is a fruit of the Holy Spirit, which is an unearned gift, but you need to stay mindful of it. It's a day to day awareness of the goodness of God in your life. If you ever forget what those things are, just start making a mental list of blessings and thanking God for each one, no matter how small they may seem. I bet you can't finish that list! I do that when I get in a mad mood (which rarely happens anymore) and before I know it, I'm joyful again. Remember Psalm 34:14, "Seek peace and pursue it"? (Peace is another fruit of the Holy Spirit.) The same could be said for joy. "Seek joy and pursue it."

MY SOUL REJOICES IN SALVATION

"And my soul shall be joyful in the Lord; **it shall rejoice in His salvation."** *Psalm 35:9*

Salvation means deliverance, rescue, welfare, help. Eternal life is one of the benefits of salvation, but it doesn't begin when your body dies. It begins when your spirit dies. (Gal.2:20) The moment you receive Jesus Christ as your Lord and Savior, that's when your eternal life begins. Along with it comes the manifestation of salvation in your life. It doesn't drop out of the sky all at once, and it isn't handed to you on a silver platter. You still have to do certain things and God doesn't usually do it all at once, because He doesn't want you to think that you did it without Him. If you get prideful about the things you experience with God, chances are you may think you don't need Him anymore. He wants the glory for your life, and He deserves it. My best day trying to handle things on my own was pathetic compared to any day that God was in submitted control of. I was undoubtedly my own worst enemy. Trying to do things without God is like trying to put yourself in the place of God. I am all too aware of my own limitations, but God doesn't have any limitations and He delights in the salvation of His people. Divine healing, prosperity, loving relationships, charity, peace, and wisdom naturally result in a response of immense gladness. A friend of mine was on dialysis for years. I remember the day she got the call saying that a kidney had been found for her. She had to leave for the hospital immediately. Every person there with her was rejoicing. When she came home a few days later, you couldn't even tell that she had had surgery. But she was *rejoicing*, and so was everyone there waiting for her. We were shouting and praising God and clapping. It was a time of rejoicing in the Lord. She had trusted God for years, and never complained or doubted or spoke contrary to what the Word says about God helping her and saving her and comforting her. And He did it. And she's perfectly healthy. No one else could have assured her of her health. No one else could have healed her that fast. God did that. She didn't do it. The doctors didn't do it. God did it. I know that there's something you can think of to rejoice in, even if you haven't seen it come to pass. Go ahead and rejoice now, in faith.

I AM ABUNDANTLY SATISFIED WITH THE FULLNESS OF GOD'S HOUSE

"They are abundantly satisfied with the fullness of Your house, and You give them drink from the river of Your pleasures." Psalm 36:8

Who is it that is abundantly satisfied with all the fullness of God's house? Those who put their trust in Him. (Ps. 36:7) Those who trust in God drink freely from the fountain of life. (Ps. 36:9) I often think of it as being held underwater, drowning, unable to breathe, lost in the darkness, flailing to exhaustion, and finally coming up out of the waters, into light, my lungs filling with air, life permeating my body. That's how it feels to me. Psalm 36:9 also says, "In Your light we see light." I didn't even know I was in darkness until I came into light. I went to hand out food from the ministry to an area that I had grown up in. All my life, I had thought of the place as being dark, even in the daytime. I never understood why. I knew that it was a "bad area", but never connected that with the darkness that hovered over it. That day, I noticed something that I had never seen before. We went to a house where a man and woman were sitting outside. The color of the woman's eyes seemed to be black, like they were totally pupils. The man sitting with her didn't budge to help her carry the food, so we helped her take it to the door. We weren't

145

allowed to go inside. I discerned that she was abused, physically and mentally controlled by the man. When I got back in the truck, I mentioned it to the other woman I was with. She confirmed that it was true, that she had tried to get the woman to leave and come to the ministry, but she wouldn't. The next place we came to had several people sitting in the yard. I walked over to them, and on the back side of the group, I saw a woman that I knew. She was a drug addict and had actually just gotten out of prison, but she was still a beautiful woman. However, I noticed that her eyes looked just like the other woman's. The color was completely black. She didn't seem to be on drugs at the time. Every place we went in that neighborhood, *everyone's eyes looked like that*. And I know that some of those people weren't drug users, because I knew them. I had always seen the darkness *over* the place, but I didn't see the darkness in the people until God delivered me from it. I realized that *I used to be one of those people* and I had no idea! You are a child of Light. (Jn. 12:36, 1 Thes. 5:4-5) You are the temple of God. (1 Cor. 6:19) Shine bright with the all the fullness of the Light of the World.

I DRINK FROM THE RIVER OF GOD'S PLEASURES

"They are abundantly satisfied with the fullness of Your house, and **You give them drink from the river of Your pleasures."** *Psalm 36:8*

God Himself is the fountain of life. God's own Holy Spirit is the Living Water, which flows freely from every person whose heart believes in Jesus. (Jn. 7:38-39) The Hebrew word for "pleasures" is Beth-Eden, which translates to "house of bliss", or "house of Eden". Eden was the garden where Adam and Eve were, where every need was provided for, where Adam walked with God in the cool of the day, a place of abundance. In Scripture, Paradise is synonymous with Heaven. (Lk. 23:43) What if, right now, God took you to His house, gave you a set of keys, and told you to make yourself at home, and if you needed anything, just let Him know? That's exactly what He did! When you truly grasp God's powerful, intricate, meticulous, abounding, unfailing, unconditional love for you, you will find that there's nothing else that can quench your craving but *Him*. The other things just don't matter anymore. And He is more than pleased to give you more of Him. He gave you His Holy Spirit to do that. From His Spirit, which lives inside you, flow rivers of life giving water that never run dry. Eden was Paradise. You can live in Paradise right here, right now. Your eternal life began the moment you received Jesus into your heart. You don't have to wait until your body expires to live in Paradise. You can drink freely from the river of God's delight *right now*. Paradise is a place of total contentment, fulfillment, and provision, a place of continuous dwelling in the very presence of God. Are you thirsty? Ask God to give you a drink from the rivers of His pleasures then get in your Word, get on your knees, listen to some worship music, and expect God's Presence.

I TRUST IN THE LORD

*"**Trust in the Lord**, and do good; dwell in the land, and feed on His faithfulness." Psalm 37:3*

This may seem like a simple instruction, but I want you to say this confession, not just today, but every day. It needs to become a part of who you are, in every sense. Even people who have been Christians many years make the mistake of giving a thing over to God, and in the next breath, taking it right back from Him. For example, someone may say, "I've been having trouble with my back, but I'm trusting God to heal me." And five minutes later, another person comes in the room and asks, "How's it going?" And the person responds with, "Oh, I'm fine, but my back is killing me!" Don't ever do that. Don't ever say *anything* is killing you! But be aware, when you are believing in God, that you don't lay it at the Cross and keep picking it back up. Give it over to God, whatever it is, and from that point on, when you think about what you laid down, thank God *in advance* for delivering you. I was in a relationship for a long time that was toxic and abusive. I never could figure out why we were even still together, but we stayed together anyway. After I had been diagnosed with a lot of things that made it look as though I probably wouldn't live much longer, I found out he had done some things specifically against me, but also against my employer, who had never done anything except go out of his way to help us. That was the final straw. I cried out and asked God to get my boyfriend away from me, and He did. It took a few weeks to get myself together and relocate, but every time I thought about that man, I'd say, "Oops, God! Sorry. That's Yours. Take it back." And I was able to never go back to him again. But in that time, I poured into the Word. I spent a lot of time with Jesus. And even though I had no idea where I was going or what I was going to do or how I was going to do it, *I put my full and total trust in God.* I didn't worry or overthink. I didn't even put forth a lot of effort into where I would go, but when the time came, the place I had been checking into fell flat and God put a place in front of me that was in His plan all along, and it was perfect. I can honestly and confidently say that I am a person who trusts God with the big things and the little things. He has *always* been faithful and sure to take care of me far better than I could even care for myself, even before I knew Him. I want *you* to live a life of full confidence in God, too, so make this confession a part of everything that concerns you.

I DO GOOD

*"Trust in the Lord, and **do good**; dwell in the land, and feed on His faithfulness." Psalm 37:3*

Acts 10:38 says Jesus went around doing good. I've always loved that. It makes me want to go around doing good, too. I get a mental image of Jesus skipping around, throwing blessings around like confetti. I looked up the word "good" in Hebrew and in Greek and it wasn't any specific thing. It basically meant "good works". But in Acts 10:38, it does specify what kind of good works Jesus did. It says "healing all who were oppressed by the devil". Those words mean exactly what they say, too, but in English, we have certain ideas about what those words are limited to. Let me explain each one. Healing isn't limited to illness. Healing means to be made whole. Deliverance. To be set free. All means ALL. That means there are no special favorites. It's for everybody. Oppressed means under the control of. And the devil is just the devil. He's already been defeated by Jesus at the Cross and his time is ending and he knows it, so he's mad as hell and wants to take as many people as he can there with him. And he sucks. This is where you come in. You pick up where Jesus left off, *doing good.* Everything you do on this earth in love, kindness, charity, peace, compassion, is doing good. Whatever you do in the will and love of God is doing good. And if you can lead someone to Christ, that is amazing good! If you can help someone break free from addiction, abuse, pride, greed, any works of the flesh or spiritual bondage, you are doing good. If you volunteer at your church, at a nursing home, delivering meals to the homeless, having Bible study at the county jail, spending time with women at a domestic violence shelter, whatever you do, wherever you do it, if it's from your heart and it's God's will, *you are doing*

151

good. Praying for someone is doing good. Keeping your mouth shut and walking away from someone who is trying to provoke you is doing good. Romans 12:21 says not to be overcome by evil, but to *overcome evil with good*! That's God's will and that's God's *way*. That's Jesus' way! Remember He said, "I am THE WAY". (Jn. 14:6) *This* is how He lives inside you. *This* is how you are the hands and feet of Jesus. *This* is how you do good.

I DWELL IN THE LAND

"Trust in the Lord, and do good; **dwell in the land**, *and feed on His faithfulness." Psalm 37:3*

The two things I have always wanted, besides love, is security and safety. It seemed like all three of these things came so easily, even by default, to most people, but somehow they always escaped me. God gives His Word, that if you trust Him and do good things that are pleasing to Him, that you will most definitely see the goodness of the Lord in the land of the living. (Ps. 27:13-14) It doesn't mean that you won't have troubles or that your life will suddenly become perfect, but when things get out of hand, God will be right there with you and He will make a way out of no way (Is. 43:19) and everything will work together for your good. (Rom. 8:28) It's a hard reality, but some of the biggest, best blessings come in the form of adversity. Blessings in disguise. When something happens that seems impossible to survive, or just too much to handle, God says that if you trust Him, and in *all* your ways acknowledge Him, He will direct your path. (Prov. 3:5) And while you are waiting, overcome evil with good. (Rom. 12:21) *Then* you will dwell in the land, the land of God's peace, protection, favor, and provision. You will be in a continuous state of God's care. It is an absolute must that you remain in a constant state of intimacy and communion with Him. It is in the presence of God that you are untouchable by anything outside. It doesn't matter what's going on around you or what diseases "run in your family" or what happened to your friend's sister. It really doesn't even matter what you feel emotionally, it's what you *believe*. The smartest thing you can do in any and every situation is find out what God says and do whatever it takes to *believe His Word* and speak it every chance you get. Speak that Word to the situation until it changes. God's telling you right here, "Trust Me, do good, and I've got you!" That's how you "dwell in the land".

I FEED ON GOD'S FAITHFULNESS

*"Trust in the Lord, and do good; dwell in the land, and **feed on His faithfulness.**" Psalm 37:3*

Trust God in everything, no matter what. Do good, even when it's hard or inconvenient. *Then* you will remain in God's presence and your life will flourish. *But...* There will be times when you think maybe God forgot about you, where you don't hear from Him like you used to or you yourself may even be feeling less passionate for the things of God. This is called a dry period, and we all go through them. It's during these times that you have to stubbornly press in and keep moving forward. I have three things that help me do that. One, I remind myself that it's a test of *my faithfulness*. Two, I increase speaking God's Word, personal confessions like the ones in this devotional. The third thing I do, especially when worry or doubt raise their ugly heads, is *feed on God's faithfulness.* I remind myself of all the things He's brought me through, all that He's done for me, all that He gives me, and I thank Him. I remind myself of *who He is*. And I tell myself that no matter what it *feels like*, HE IS WITH ME AND HE IS FOR ME. I do it over and over and over. I feed on those things. Your body needs food to live. Good food provides energy and strength and growth. Junk food may taste good, but it doesn't have any benefits for your body. In fact, too much can be really bad for you. It's the same with things of Spirit. Everything in the

154

physical realm is also spiritual, so which spirit are you feeding on? And how often? You don't just eat on Sundays or holidays, so your spirit shouldn't be starved either. God told me once to "eat the Word". I took that to mean read my Bible at breakfast, lunch, and dinner, (in addition to my morning and night reading). The first day I did it, I read *instead* of eating, as part of a fast, but after the first day, I read either before or during mealtimes. When you need strength, encouragement, guidance, comfort, love, peace, whatever you need, and even if you think you don't need anything, feed on God's Word and His faithfulness. He has never and will never leave you or turn His back on you. (Deut. 31:6) You eat every day, usually several times a day, whether you feel starved or not, so do the same for your spirit. Reflect on all the times that you couldn't see your way out of a situation, and how God made a way where there seemed to be no way. That's how you feed on God's faithfulness.

I AM DESIRABLE

*"So the King **will greatly desire** your beauty; because He is your Lord, worship Him." Psalm 45:11*

Do you think of yourself as desirable? For me, that's one of the last words I would have ever used to describe myself. I always had very low self esteem, so even when I actually was desirable to someone, I never believed it. God changed that, though. I remember the first time I ever saw myself through God's eyes. It was an awesome, inexplicable transformation. It had nothing to do with looks. I still looked the same, but I knew that somehow, I looked different. Today, I believe that it was the light of Christ shining in me and through me. When you pursue holiness for the sake of pleasing God and being obedient to His Word, He will fill you with light. Light shines in the darkness (Jn. 1:5) and it helps people find their way out. (Acts 26:18) And even when it is seen from a distance, it gives hope that there really is a way out. Have you ever known anyone that was a "lost cause" that got saved and they were like a completely different person? I don't mean self righteous or judgmental, but they were transformed into another person altogether and even though they looked the same, there was just something that was undeniably different? They were radiant? That's the light I mean. That's Christ inside. That's the beauty of holiness. (1 Chron. 16:29, Ps. 29:2, Ps.

156

96:9) It's inner beauty and God values that beauty above anything the world around you tries to tell you, sell you, or otherwise make you believe. Once you see yourself through God's eyes, through the eyes of Love (1 Jn. 4:8, 1 Jn. 4:16) the eyes of the heart, (1 Sam. 16:7) you will know that you were desirable all along. If you ever doubted that, it was because you were fed lies about who you are. Your Creator desires you. That's all that matters. Your Creator knew you before you were born. He created you in your mother's womb. (Jer. 1:5) Of all God's creation, He only calls *you* His masterpiece. (Eph. 2:10) He calls *you* fearfully and wonderfully made. (Ps. 139:14) Your Creator made you in His very own image. (Gen. 1:27) He didn't do that with any of His other creations. Only you, because He created you to be His child. He gave His Son's life to make that happen. (Jn. 3:16) You may be thinking, "Yeah, but you don't know about..." I do know. I was one of those "lost causes". Some people probably still think of me that way, but I DON'T because I know GOD has *never* seen me that way. Read Ezekiel 16:4-14. It describes God's desire for all His children, no matter who they are, what they look like, where they're from, what they've done or haven't done. This is a beautiful description of God's desire for *you*.

I AM BEAUTIFUL

*"So the King will greatly desire **your beauty**; because He is your Lord, worship Him."* *Psalm 45:11*

I'm from the south, so I grew up hearing people say, "Don't be ugly. Don't act ugly. Don't talk ugly" when I was misbehaving. There's also the phrase, "God don't like ugly." None of these phrases refer to outward appearance. They refer to the behavior of a person, their inner beauty. Physical appearance is what most people base beauty on. It's what the world around us conditions us to believe, but that isn't based on God's idea of beauty. In Isaiah 53:2, it says that Jesus "has no form or comeliness; and when we see Him, there is no beauty that we should desire Him." Ezekiel 28:12 describes Lucifer (Satan) as "the seal of perfection, full of wisdom and perfect in beauty." Helen Keller is quoted as saying, "The best and most beautiful things in the world cannot be seen or even touched – they must be felt with the heart." True, real, lasting beauty comes from the heart. It comes from Christ within you. It comes from holiness, humility, the fruit of the Spirit, compassion, and servitude. Although love is one of the fruits of the Spirit, it's one that everything else depends on to flourish. 1 Corinthians 13:4-8 gives a Biblical description of love. It is patient, kind, isn't envious, isn't boastful or prideful, is not rude or self-seeking, is not provoked, thinks no evil, does not enjoy sin but instead enjoys truth, righteousness, and goodness, is tolerant, believes all things, hopes all things, endures all things. And it *never* fails. 1 Corinthians 13:1-3 lists all kinds of powerful moves of the Spirit, but it ends by saying that without love, it means nothing. 1 Peter 3:3-4 (TLB) says, "Don't be concerned about the outward beauty that depends on fancy hairstyles, expensive jewelry, or beautiful clothes. You should be known for the beauty that comes from within, the unfading beauty that comes from a gentle and quiet spirit, which is so precious to God." When I first came across this verse, I thought that was it for me. There was no way I could be gentle *and quiet, too?* Maybe I could be one or the other, sometimes, but both at the same time? *All* the time? I love that I can confidently say, "I can't, but God can." And He does. His Spirit inside you will take you there. God created you to be you, so a gentle and quiet spirit within *you* will look different than a gentle and quiet spirit in someone else, but your beauty, in all its fullness, comes from Christ's beauty, from His holiness and love, and He is inside of you. Anything that you desire more of that is from Christ, God will freely give to you. All you have to do is ask Him and believe that He will do it. It *pleases* God to manifest Christ through you. Your beauty is from the Lord Himself. It is God who makes you beautiful. "Your fame went out among the nations because of your beauty, for it was perfect *through My splendor which I bestowed on you*, says the Lord God." (Ez. 16:14) You really are beautiful.

I WORSHIP MY LORD

"So the King will greatly desire your beauty; because He is your Lord, **worship Him.***"* Psalm 45:11

I never thought of myself as a worshipper, because I'm not very expressive. In fact, I tend to be very inhibited in front of other people. I can't sing or dance well, and I know God thinks it's beautiful anyway, but in church, for instance, I don't really dance like David. (2 Sam. 6:14) I do sing, though, just not well. I used to think that my worship wasn't good enough and that I was a failure in honoring God, after all He had done for me. It felt horrible. I wanted to worship, but I was exhausted, and the awkwardness just made it worse. I knew worship wasn't supposed to be like that, so I prayed and asked God to show me how to worship Him. Later, while I was in the kitchen at the ministry, cooking for around 100 people, I was listening to a worship cd and it hit me- my service is a form of worship! In the kitchen, I regularly sang and danced and lifted my hands in worship with a big mixing spoon or knife in my hand. I asked God if He would accept my service as worship. A few days later, I was mixing something in a large bowl and imagined Jesus standing across from me with His hands in the bowl too, our hands touching as we mixed the ingredients together, *and I felt Him touch me!* Surely God had answered my prayer with a big, huge "YES!"

You see, God is the one who gave me the gift of cooking. It's something I've been doing since I was a little girl. It's something I'm passionate about. And cooking is where I flow. The kitchen is my dance floor. Every bit of that is a gift from God. Only you can say where your dance floor is. That thing that you're really good at, that you lose all sense of time and space doing, that thing that blesses others but you feel so blessed just by doing it… Use it for the glory of God. Ask God to bless you in the work of your hands, and to accept it as worship. Lay every moment that you spend on your personal dance floor on the altar in worship. That's why God gave you that gift. Something else I've done my whole life is write. In all my years, I've never finished anything until I wrote this devotional. God revealed to me the reason why… because this is the first thing I've ever written *for Him* and *His glory*. He gave you your gift to give back to Him *in worship*.

I DWELL IN THE SECRET PLACE OF THE MOST HIGH

*"He who **dwells in the secret place of the Most High** shall abide under the shadow of the Almighty." Psalm 91:1*

Psalm 91 is filled with the promises of protection God gives to those who seek Him and are obedient to Him. Dwelling in the secret place is simply abiding in that state, remaining in a state of God's protection and provision. I don't want to say this is the most important identity confession, but it is one in which a lot of others are dependant. If you can grasp that by seeking God faithfully, by being reverent toward Him and obedient to His Word, that you are under God's divine care for everything that concerns you, it will change the way you live, the way you see yourself, and the way you see others and relate to them. The thing about this identity confession is that many of the other confessions about who God created you to be is the result of this confession. The secret place is that place where it's just you and God. That place where God's presence is undeniable, where His Spirit manifests itself. It's time in prayer, time in the Word, time given to someone in need. God is there. You are his child. What could be more pleasing to your Father than to seek Him out and want to really know Him and be like Him, not just when you want something, but every day of your life? When you dwell in the secret place, it doesn't mean that sometimes bad things won't happen, but that when they do, God will always use that situation or person or thing for your good and His glory and purposes. I read a quote recently that said, "There's no crown without a Cross." It means that there's no victory without trials, no life without death, no abundance without sacrifice. Everything that Jesus accomplished for the entire human race, He did at the Cross. The Cross doesn't just define who Jesus is, it defines who you are, too. My hope is that you will make this confession one that you speak daily and that it transforms the way you live and the way you see yourself. It is what it is, regardless of how you see yourself, but when you truly can identify yourself as someone who seeks after God and therefore is under His perfect, complete care for everything that concerns you, a lot of the other things will be much easier to absorb. I've learned through my own experience that how I feel about a situation really doesn't matter, but I still have carnal thoughts and emotions sometimes. When I do, I remind myself that God is still on the throne and that He who has begun a good work in me *will* complete it until the day of Jesus Christ. (Php. 1:6)

I ABIDE UNDER THE SHADOW OF THE ALMIGHTY

*"He who dwells in the secret place of the Most High shall **abide under the shadow of the Almighty."** Psalm 91:1*

To abide means to remain, continue, or stay. One of the Hebrew definitions refers to all night. That makes me think of prayer. The longest prayers I've ever prayed always seemed to be at night. The shadow, though, is the shelter, the care, of God's protection. You can't be under a shadow unless you're close to where the shadow is coming from. To be under God's shadow, you have to be close to Him. You have to seek intimacy with Him. James 4:8 says, "Draw near to God and He will draw near to you." That means that if you seek God diligently, with a pure heart, He will manifest Himself to you. And that's His promise. I used to work two jobs, and lived with my cousin, so any time at home meant that I never had any alone time. I believe that God lined up a secret meeting, but I totally thought it was my own idea. I had the day off from both jobs, which was rare, and my cousin had to work that day, too, so I was going to be home by myself. I had the idea to have lunch with Jesus, like a date. I put music on while I was making the food. I talked to Jesus. When I sat down to eat, I was still talking like He was sitting across from me. I even would hold up food for Him to eat. Suddenly a song came on that I really liked, so I got up to dance for Jesus. I thought. While I was singing and dancing, I realized that I was not dancing *for* Jesus, I was dancing *with Him*! I fell to the floor! And when I did, I had a vision of a vision that I had had when I was 12 years old. I had forgotten about it, but it was the most significant vision I've ever had, and Jesus showed it to me again. And the realization that Jesus was there, *actually there, dancing with me*, was the most amazing thing ever in my whole life. When I moved to Texas a couple of years later, I was sitting in the car listening to the radio and heard a song where the man was singing about dancing with Jesus, and I thought, "Jesus, you danced with Him, too?" I was blown away all over again. Jesus was and is fully Man and fully God, fully King and fully Servant, fully real and alive. And you are fully *His*. You live under the shadow of His protection, provision, favor, and perfect love, at all times, in every circumstance. No exceptions. Nothing is too hard for Him. (Jer. 32:27) Jesus is the Name above *EVERY* name. (Php. 2:9) At the Name of Jesus, EVERY knee will bow. (Php. 2:10) The knees of sickness, poverty, abuse, addiction, pride, lust, greed, whatever you can name, will bow at the Name of Jesus, the Name whose shadow covers you, protects you, and shelters you from any and every storm, situation, stronghold, fear, or pain that you can think of. Jesus covers you with His love.

THE LORD IS MY REFUGE AND MY FORTRESS

*"I will say of **the Lord, "He is my Refuge and my Fortress**; my God, in Him I will trust.""* Psalm 91:2

The Lord is your Refuge and your Fortress. He is your place of safety, protection, and provision.. In Him, you are untouchable. Whatever tries to come against you may still come, but a lot of it won't and what does come is under God's control. The Bible doesn't promise that you won't go through trials, but that in the midst of them, God will be with you and fight for you. (Jn. 16:33) A refuge is a place of safety. A fortress is a place that is walled in, a stronghold for protection, such as walls around a city. Another definition of fortress is "a person or thing not susceptible to outside influence or disturbance." Habakkuk 3:17-19 says, "Though the fig tree may not blossom, nor fruit be on the vines; though the labor of the olive may fail, and the fields yield no food; though the flock may be cut off from the fold, and there be no herd in the stalls- yet I will rejoice in the God of my salvation. The Lord God is my strength; He will make my feet like deer's feet, and He will make me walk on my high hills." That means that no matter what's going on in the world around you, you are not a part of that. You are different. You are God's people. The economy may be down, but your needs are met. There may be a virus going around, but it doesn't touch you. Another definition I found for the word fortress that really intrigued me was "a place to prepare for battle." God equips you for every battle you will ever face through His Word. It's important to get that Word into your spirit. You may think it isn't doing anything, but when you need it, the Holy Spirit will bring it to your remembrance so that you can speak it into existence. "Now when they bring you to the synagogues and magistrates and authorities, do not worry about how or what you should answer, or what you should say. For the Holy Spirit will teach you in that very hour what you ought to say." (Lk. 12:11) You may think, "Synagogues? Magistrates and authorities? What?" Ephesians 6:12 explains it like this, "For we do not wrestle against flesh and blood, but against principalities, against powers, against the rulers of the darkness of this age, against spiritual hosts of wickedness in the heavenly places." The synagogue of Satan is referred to in Revelation 2:9 and 3:9. It's talking about people who were persecuting the church, who say they are Jews but are not. In other words, those who opposed Jesus or were trying to appear religious but their hearts and actions proved otherwise. Spiritual warfare is real. The things that you can't see are more real than the things you can see, because they're eternal. They're forever. Christ coming to earth as a man, dying on the Cross, and being resurrected was the means by which Satan was defeated, and the means by which Jesus gave you authority over Satan. "Behold, I give you the authority to trample on serpents and scorpions, and over *all* the power of the enemy, and *nothing* shall by any means hurt you." Believing in the truth of God's Word, trusting in God to do it, and staying in the presence of God through prayer and His Word,

167

applying it to every aspect of your life- those are the laws of the land behind the walls of the secret place of the Most High.

I TRUST IN MY GOD

*"I will say of the Lord, "He is my Refuge and my Fortress; **my God, in Him I will trust.**" Psalm 91:2*

I've never understood people that *don't* have trust issues, probably because I've always had them. Jesus says in Matthew 10:16, "Be wise as serpents and harmless as doves." My pastor says, "You're covered in the Blood, but you still have to use wisdom." But when it comes to trusting God, the Bible says, "Trust in the Lord with all your heart, and lean not on your own understanding." (Prov. 3:5) For me, that took some practice. It wasn't like, "Okay, the Bible says do that, so I'm going to do it." When you've spent a lifetime having your trust betrayed at every turn, it's hard to place your full trust in someone, especially if you haven't known that person very long. From my own experience, I can tell you that God can be fully trusted at all times in every circumstance. The way I got to that conclusion was by getting to know Him, by spending time with Him, in His Word, in prayer, in worship and serving Him. Even then, sometimes I still had trust issues, not because I didn't trust in *His* ability, but because I didn't think that *I* was good enough. I knew that God could do anything for *other people*, but they probably hadn't done the things I had done or lived the way I lived or been through the things I had been through. Two things changed that for me. One, when I think back on all the times God has been faithful, it's beyond my ability to count. He has *never* failed me. Two, the presence of the Holy Spirit living inside me. The Bible calls Him the "guarantee" of everything that God promises. (2 Cor. 1:22) The devil tries to slip thoughts into people's minds that question the Word of God. If that happens to you, remember that you have experienced the Holy Spirit, and nothing or nobody can convince you otherwise. The Holy Spirit also gives you discernment, to know things that you would have no other way of knowing. This is sometimes called intuition or sixth sense by the world's standards, but I want to give credit where credit is due. It's the Holy Spirit, living inside of *you*.

I AM THE SHEEP OF GOD'S PASTURE

*"Know that the Lord, He is God; it is He who has made us, and not we ourselves; we are His people and **the sheep of His pasture**." Psalm 100:3*

My mother used to call me her little lamb. Now I'm the sheep of God's pasture. The Bible refers to Jesus as the Good Shepherd. (Jn. 10:11, 14) So by being His sheep, you are under His complete care. Sheep need a shepherd, as opposed to living in the wild, because they are not very smart animals. They are also very fearful animals. Even something as harmless as the sound of running water will scare a sheep. Sheep are defenseless on their own. In groups, they have a better chance of protection, but they are also easily scattered. When a sheep falls into a ditch and lands on its back, it can't get back up, especially if their wool hasn't been shorn in a while. Their bodies are too heavy and their legs are basically just little skinny, stick-like protrusions. Being in this state is called being "cast down". It's referred to several times in the Bible in regard to overthrowing evil forces and even sorrow. (Ps. 42:11) Sheep recognize their shepherd's voice and won't go with just anybody. (Jn. 10:27) They do create friendships and appear to be loyal. They're emotional creatures, too, capable of mourning for their sheep friends when they die and building loving relationships. Another interesting similarity between sheep and people- sheep are not meant to carry burdens. (Ps. 55:22) Sheep don't have reasoning skills to enable them to do what's best for them, but instead will do what's most convenient or immediate. Sheep really aren't that much different from a lot of humans. I want you to read over Psalm 23, then re-read it, using your name instead of "my", "I", or "me". You may even want to write it out that way, and read it out loud every day. The Bible says that a hired shepherd will abandon his sheep, but Jesus is the Good Shepherd. He loves His sheep and will lay His life down for them. He did that for you, little lamb.

I SEEK GOD WITH MY WHOLE HEART

*"Blessed are those who keep His testimonies, **who seek Him with the whole heart.**" Psalm 119:2*

"And you will seek Me and find Me when you search for Me with all your heart." (Jer. 29:13) A real, live relationship with God will most certainly bring peace and joy like you've never known. I'm not talking about filling space on a seat in church every Sunday. I'm talking about really going after God Himself. His Word, His ways, His touch, His voice. The word "heart" here can be translated as "mind, understanding, wisdom". Seeking on that level takes time and an intentional, steady focus. It means giving your attention to the Word of God, to prayer, to studying and applying the Word as you understand it. It means going deep, going hard, going full force with hunger in your heart. You're going to have to lay everything else aside and push through, but God promises to meet you and to give you a testimony of what that looks like in your life. I often stop and close my eyes and remind myself that God is with me and in me. I wait until I am aware of His presence, then I resume whatever I was doing. I know that there are times when I can feel the Spirit, but I have to remind myself that even when I don't feel Him, He is there. That gives me peace. It gives me strength. It gives me comfort. I seek God in times of trouble, but that's because I also seek Him in my day to day, not the other way around. My hope for you is that you also seek God in your day to day, in the little things, in everything. Don't seek Him only when you want something or you're in trouble. He's already there. Seek Him to know Him. He's your Father, your Lord and King. He gave His only Son's life to make you His child. He is worthy of all praise, and glory, and honor, and He is worthy of your time and attention, too.

I WALK IN GOD'S WAYS

*"They also do no iniquity; **they walk in His ways**." Psalm 119:3*

"But be doers of the Word, and not hearers only, deceiving yourselves." (Jms. 1:22) There are a lot of people that don't want anything to do with the church. For all the many reasons, I know that one of the biggest reasons is "religious people". I've known people all my life that went to church faithfully, could quote Scripture, but were mean spirited, judgmental, hypocritical, and legalistic. Religion is an evil spirit. Relationship is an experience, a way of life. Psalm 119:3 refers to conforming to the image of Christ, not because God is a mean Father that's waiting for you to mess up so He can punish you, but rather it's wanting to conform to the image of Christ because He sacrificed His life so that you would be blameless and spend eternal life in Heaven with Him, and because you love Him and want to please Him. Walking in God's ways doesn't mean beating people over the head with your Bible. It means holding their hand in prayer, handing out food, giving of your time and mercy and compassion, It means walking in love. Yes, it means giving up a lot of things, even though "everybody is doing it", even though it isn't technically illegal, but it's either immoral or questionable, at best. Walking in God's ways requires you to do the right thing, even if no one else will ever know. God knows and so do you. God wants you to walk in His ways for His glory, but also for your own good and the greater good of those around you. The things you give up to do that will become less desirable anyway, because the things you gain are so much greater. Any time I think of something I no longer do, I immediately remind myself that it isn't worth exchanging anything in my life that God has blessed me with. My worst day now is a thousand times better than my best day before I knew Jesus.

I PRAISE GOD WITH UPRIGHTNESS OF HEART

"I will praise you with uprightness of heart, when I learn your righteous judgments." Psalm 119:7

To praise God with uprightness of heart is to offer sincere thanks with all your heart. It's the manner in which you offer thanks, praising God with your whole being. It's lifting up the sacrifice of praise with your mind and understanding, with an awareness of all He has done for you. Psalm 9:1 says, "I will praise You, O Lord, with my whole heart; I will tell of all your marvelous works." One of the definitions in the Greek for the word "praise" in this verse is "confess". Not only will your praise be a confession of thanksgiving to God, but to others of His goodness, His mercy, His faithfulness, His peace, and His love. This is where your confession, your testimony, holds power. Revelation 12:11 says, "And they overcame him by the Blood of the Lamb and by the word of their testimony, and they did not love their lives to the death." Jesus shed His Blood on the Cross and defeated Satan and death. *Your testimony* serves to overcome the devil until he is banished from the earth. God is worthy of all praise and that should pour forth in everything that you think, do, and say. It takes intentional, constant focus. With your mind, you have to redirect to His goodness, His presence, and His

Word. You have to live out His Word. To live it out, you have to search it out. You have to know it. The Word of God is alive inside of you. (Heb. 4:12) You may not think you have a lot of Scripture memorized, but the Holy Spirit will remind you when you need it. In your daily life, the Holy Spirit will convict you, or move you, to live according to the Word. You will just know that you know what is righteous and just and pleasing to God. And you will know what isn't. Following that unction is walking by God's Spirit. Praise God by praying the Psalms back to Him. Give Him your heartfelt thanks, and tell those around you what He's done for you. *You*, my brother or sister, are an overcomer. Go look at yourself in the mirror and declare, "I am an overcomer, in the mighty Name of Jesus!" Praise the Lord!

I HAVE HIDDEN GOD'S WORD IN MY HEART

*"**Your Word I have hidden in my heart**, that I might not sin against You." Psalm 119:11*

God gives us His Word to instruct us how to live. That's why you have to be diligent to read and study His Word, so that when you are faced with sin, you will know how to handle it. Each model of cell phones is different from the others, just like every person is different. All cell phones come with a user manual specific to that phone's functions. You can toss the manual aside and figure it out by trial and error, or you can read and apply the instructions in the manual. What works for one cell phone may not work for another one, but there are general instructions that apply to all phones. God gives you His Word as your own personal user manual. The instructions are the same for everyone, but God will guide you with personal instructions by His Spirit, based on His Word. You don't have to memorize the entire Bible, but memorization is beneficial. Based on the amount of time and thought you put into the Word, the Holy Spirit will pull it up as you need it, whether you think you know it or not. This comes during times of prayer, when you are witnessing to someone, or even as a thought in your own voice. The way you know that it's the Holy Spirit and not your own thought is testing it against the Word itself. God's will is His Word and He will never tell you something that doesn't line up with His Word. Hide the Word as a treasure within your heart. Meditate on the Word. Ponder over it. Pray over it. Speak it. You know, the Word of God is a weapon. You wouldn't walk around in enemy territory with your sword drawn. That would be inviting trouble. Knowing that you had a sword, a *living Sword*, hidden and within easy reach, would enable you to confidently handle attacks. Whatever we fill ourselves with overflows. This is what the Bible means by "rivers of living water". (Jn. 7:38-39) The Holy Spirit living within you will pour Himself out of you when you fill yourself with His Word.

MY EYES HAVE BEEN OPENED TO SEE WONDROUS THINGS IN GOD'S WORD

"Open my eyes to see wondrous things from Your law."   Psalm
119:18

The Bible is beautifully layered. There appears to be a particular meaning on the surface, but as you read the same things over again, they have another meaning, and yet another. The Bible has many purposes- teaching, guidance, instruction, encouragement, empowerment, warfare, worship, correction, it goes on and on. The human mind cannot comprehend the Bible on its own. With each new layer, it becomes necessary to have a new understanding. The deeper the layer, the less the flesh can comprehend. It is only possible by the Spirit, and even then, it isn't until God opens our spiritual eyes, our spiritual understanding, to receive them. In 2 Kings 6:16, Elisha and his servant were surrounded by an army of Syrian soldiers. Verse 17 says, "And Elisha prayed, and said, "Lord, I pray, open his eyes that he may see." Then the Lord opened the eyes of the young man, and he saw. And behold, the mountain was full of horses and chariots of fire all around Elisha." God opened Elisha's servant's eyes to see things in the spiritual realm that were not visible to the eyes of the flesh. The spiritual realm is far more real than the physical realm because it's eternal. It's forever. The things of the spirit can only be revealed by the Spirit. The Spirit is alive inside of you, so those things are possible within you, too. I have a sticky note on the inside cover of my Bible, and I simply wrote it on the inside cover of another Bible, that reads "Open my eyes to see wondrous things in Your Word". I try to remember to say that before every Bible reading. God graciously reveals His deep secrets because not only does He want you to live according to His Word, you are the child of the Author of those Words. He wants you to live like Him, talk like Him, think like Him, love like Him. (Eph. 5:1) I tried for most of my life to read the Bible, but I couldn't comprehend or even remember anything I read. My reading comprehension and understanding has always been above average, but it wasn't until God *opened my eyes*, my spiritual understanding, (what is also called the eyes of my heart,) that I could understand anything beyond the basics that a child may understand. Once He opened up the Scriptures for me, the Bible not only made sense, it came alive to me. It spoke to *me*, in my day to day, right here, right now experiences. For lack of a better term, my eyes continue to widen, my spiritual vision becomes clearer and refocuses, as does my life. Make it a habit to ask God to open your eyes to see wondrous things in His Word each time you read your Bible. You will be blown away. God is SO AWESOME!

I AM REVIVED ACCORDING TO GOD'S WORD

*"My soul clings to the dust; **revive me according to Your Word**."*
Psalm 119:25

"Revive" means "to restore to life, to restore from a depressed, inactive, or unused state, to bring back to life". The Word of God can literally do that. It can restore life to a dead body. (Jn. 11:43-44) The Word of God can revive your soul when you are experiencing spiritual dryness. (Ps. 119:25) The Word of God can restore dead situations, things that have died away. (Rom. 4:17) In other words, don't ever say never. In Ezekiel 16:4-8, God tells Ezekiel through a vision to prophesy to dry bones, telling them to live. They became flesh and rose up as an army. The word "prophesy" doesn't necessarily mean to foretell future events. It means to speak the Word of God over a person, a place, a situation, *yourself*, and thereby call those things that be not as though they were. That's how God created the world and everything in it, by speaking it into existence as though it already existed. (Gen. 1 & 2) Remember, God watches over His Word to perform it. It *never* comes back to Him void. It accomplishes what it was sent forth to do. (Jer. 1:12, Is. 55:11) Whatever looks dead in your life, God can raise it to new life. No matter how you feel, what it looks like, who says what, what you think, God can restore you to victorious, joy-filled life. Nothing can stand against the power of God. (2 Chron. 20:6) NOTHING. Christine Caine is quoted in her inspirational blog Propel as saying, "Impossible is where God starts. Miracles are what He does." That is so powerful. When you truly realize how big God is, it will radically change your prayer life, your faith, your life, and the lives of everyone you come in contact with. The same God that gave you life can most definitely revive life within you.

I AM STRENGTHENED BY GOD'S WORD

"My soul melts from heaviness; **strengthen me according to Your Word."** *Psalm 119:28*

Heaviness refers to sorrow. It's also an evil spirit. Many of the Psalms speak of depression, using the words "downcast", "brokenhearted", "mourning". David experienced depression from guilt over sin. (Ps. 38:4). In 2 Samuel 12, he mourned the deaths of two of his sons. In Psalm 42, David is in the midst of all kinds of trouble and desperately wants to hear from God. According to Mental Health America, major depression is one of the most common mental illnesses, affecting over 16 million American adults each year. That's adults only. According to the Word of God, depression isn't a mental illness, but rather, it's a demonic spirit. (Is. 61:3) You have to fight spiritual battles with the Spirit. (Eph. 6:12) The greatest imagination or experience or medicine humanly conceivable doesn't even begin to compare to the love, hope, courage, peace, comfort, strength, and healing found in the Bible. Far from being merely words on a page, the Word of God is living and active. The Word of God is the Spirit of the Living Christ. (Jn. 1:1) Jesus said, "Heaven and earth will pass away, but My Words will *by no means* pass away." (Mt. 24:35, Mk. 13:31, Lk. 21:33) The source of your strength is eternal. The Living Word of God, Jesus

Christ, has already paid for your deliverance from any and every thing that can be named. (Php. 2:10) There is true freedom within the pages of the Bible. (Jn. 8:32) It is not God's will for His children to live poor, defeated, miserable lives. How does that glorify Him? You can always, always, always find strength for any and every situation, emotion, or mindset in the Word. Proverbs 12:25 says, "Anxiety in the heart of man causes depression, but a *good word* makes it glad." The Bible is that good Word. Run to it first. Run to it last. How do you get your body stronger? By exercising it, right? You have to exercise your spirit, too. It doesn't happen overnight, but there is immediate relief. Over time, your spirit man will become strong, but realize that it's in your weakness that you are strongest, because that's when you've exhausted your own resources and you have no other choice except to cry out before the Lord. Do you think He's going to say, "Oh, *now* you want My help?" Of course not! He will give you the strength you need to make it through every circumstance, and He will sustain you far beyond that. The Holy Spirit will take that Word that you have been reading and speak to you through it, even if you think you don't know it. You are never alone. You are loved, and you have everything you need to live a happy, joyous, and free life. Read Ephesians 6:10-20. STAND on the Word. Live by the TRUTH of the Word. Be a doer of the RIGHTEOUSNESS of the Word. Minister the PEACE of the Word everywhere you go. Have fearless FAITH in the Word. Put on the SALVATION of the Word every single day. Carry your SWORD (your Bible) with you at all times, and USE IT. PRAY the Word.

SPEAK (prophesy) the Word. YOU ARE STRONGER THAN EVER!

I HAVE CHOSEN THE WAY OF TRUTH

"I have chosen the way of truth; Your judgments I have laid before me." Psalm 119:30

Truth is a choice, one that you have complete control over. God gives us free will to make the choices that we want to. (Mt. 23:37) You can know what's right, but it doesn't amount to much if you don't do what's right. Believe it or not, a whole lot of people don't get that part. They think that the Bible doesn't apply to *them*, that it's meant for everybody else or just for the people back during the time it was written. To choose Truth, you have to first of all know what the Truth is. Then you have to submit to the Truth. (Jms. 4:7) You can't live like Christ without Christ, who is *the Word of God*. The power of God, the same power that raised Christ from the Cross, lives inside of you. (Rom. 6:10-11) That power is the free, unearned gift of the Holy Spirit, but it's accessed by making the conscious choice to follow the Truth found in the Word. Jesus says in John 14:6, "I am the Way, the *Truth*, and the Life." Jesus is the Word. (Jn. 1:1) Get into the Word. Stay in the Word. Feed on it like your life depends on it, because *it does!* When you abide in the Word, you are abiding in Christ. "Abide in Me (the Word) and I (the Word) in you. As the branch cannot bear fruit of itself, unless it abides in the vine, neither can you, unless you abide in Me (the Word). (Jn. 15:4) The

188

way of Truth bears fruit, based on the Word inside of you. In Psalm 119:30, the word "judgments" can be translated to "laws", or more simply "ways". When you make the choice to trust God fully and follow His ways, your life will unfold according to His plans and purposes for your life. (Prov. 3:5-6, Jer. 29:11) You don't have to plan it out. You simply have to trust Him and follow His lead. The Word (Christ) will lead you and produce fruit, for your good and His glory. You will be able to do things you've never been able to do. You will find your needs met, even when you can't logically explain it. And you will be transformed in the process. (Rom. 12:2) Choosing to follow God's ways can be intimidating at first, but God promises to help you. (Is. 41:10) God will never lead you to do anything that He knows you can't do. Making the choice to follow God *and* His ways is the way of Truth and it's the way to abundant life. You may have to give up things, people, places, beliefs, but they will be replaced with things, people, places, and beliefs that are far above anything you can ask, speak, or imagine. That's a promise. (Eph. 3:20) My sincere prayer for you is that you make the choice to follow God *and* His ways, which are found in His Word. I believe in you, because I believe in God, and nothing is impossible with Him. (Lk. 1:37) *You* are strong. (Php. 4:13) *You* are chosen. (Is. 43:10) *You* are called according to God's purpose. (Rom. 8:28) I urge you to make the choice today, *right now*, to consume the Word, submit to the Word and submit to its ways, minute by minute, day by day, and see where you are a year from now.

I TRUST IN GOD'S WORD

*"So shall I have an answer for him who reproaches me, **for I trust in Your Word.**" Psalm 119:42*

I could fill volumes with my own experiences on trusting God's Word, and I could list every Scripture in the Bible on trusting God, but today I want to share some insightful quotes from others on trusting God and His Word.

"Never be afraid to trust an unknown future to a known God." – Corrie Ten Boom

"Let your life reflect the faith you have in God. Fear nothing and pray about everything. Be strong, trust God's Word, and trust the process." – Germany Kent

"Faith isn't the ability to believe long and far into the misty future. It's simply taking God at His Word and taking the next step." – Joni Erikson Tada

"Trusting God does not mean believing He will do what you want, but rather believing He will do everything He knows is good." – Ken Sande

"When God takes out the trash, don't go digging back through it. Trust Him." – Amaka Imani Nkosazana

"Dedication is writing your name on the bottom of a blank sheet of paper and handing it to the Lord for Him to fill in." – Rick Renner

"Faith doesn't come in a bushel basket, Missy. It comes one step at a time. Decide to trust Him for one little thing today, and before you know it, you find out He's so trustworthy you be putting your whole life in His hands." – Lynn Austin

"The more you believe and trust God, the more limitless your possibilities become for your family, your career, your life." – Rick Warren

"God knows how to turn things around. He can turn your sorrow into joy – just let Him in." – Richard Daly

"By reading the Bible we learn more about God. The more we learn of Him the more we love and trust Him." – Jason A. Ponzio

"We are not worthy of His love, yet because we trust Him, it is our inheritance." – Donna Schmier

I AM FEARFULLY AND WONDERFULLY MADE

*"I will praise You, for **I am fearfully and wonderfully made**; marvelous are Your works, and that my soul knows very well."*
Psalm 139:14

I had low self esteem my whole life. Along with that came a very low self image. Even when others complimented me, I thought they were just being nice or wanted something. I even had one person tell me, "I wish you were the person on the inside that you look like on the outside." Finding out who God says that I am and knowing that what He says about me is the only Truth, and that anything that contradicts that is a lie, I no longer have low self esteem or a low self image. That doesn't mean that I think too highly of myself. It just means that I know who I am, a child of the Living God, and anything praiseworthy in me is because of Him. King David asked God, "What is man that You are mindful of him, and the son of man that You visit him? For You have made him a little lower than the angels, and You crowned him with glory and honor." (Ps. 8:4-5) The best and brightest minds in all of history can't explain the complexity of creation in all its forms, or even any of its forms. Only the Creator knows those things. In Hebrew, the word "fearfully" means "with great reverence, heart-felt interest, and respect". The word "wonderfully" means "unique, set apart". God made you with love, from His heart, for Himself. Not only did He make every part of your body, He made your mind, your emotions, your intellect, your talents, your likes and dislikes. He knows exactly how many hairs are on your head. (Lk. 12:7) He knows you thoroughly, inside and out, past, present, and future. Love created you. (1 Jn. 4:8, 16) Love has your name tattooed on the palm of His hand. (Is. 49:16) Did you know that the very breath of God is what gave you life? It's *His breath* in your lungs *right now.* (Gen. 2:7) No matter what you've ever done or not done, what you look like, how much money you have or don't have, how smart you are or aren't, *you most certainly are fearfully and wonderfully made!* You are loved beyond measure and you were created in the image of Almighty God. You are His masterpiece! Those are *His Words*, not mine. (Eph. 2:10) Ask God to let you see yourself through His eyes, the way that He looks at you, the way He loves you, and never ever forget it, because *that* is who you are.

I AM FAVORED BY BOTH GOD AND MAN

*"And so find **favor** and high esteem **in the sight of both God and man.**" Proverbs 3:4*

Favor is when people you don't know or who don't even like you do good things for you because there's just "something" about you that makes them feel the urge to do so. Favor comes from God alone, even the favor from people. It is God who turns those hearts to you. God can do all things, but He often uses people to do things through, and not necessarily "holy" type people. In Numbers 22:20-39, God used a donkey to speak to Balaam when the Angel of the Lord was blocking the way they were traveling. If God can use a donkey, he can use anybody or anything. Have you ever had someone that you know didn't like you say, "I don't know why I'm doing this..." and then do something good for you, for no explicable reason? That's the favor of God. God wants you to live an abundant life. (Jn. 10:10) It's important to trust God when it isn't easy, when things look like anything but what an abundant life looks like in your mind, because trusting God during times of trials and testing and striving to walk in His ways in the face of adversity are what get you ready for an outpouring of favor. "Therefore, my dear brothers and sisters, stand firm. Let nothing move you. Always give yourselves fully to the work of the Lord, because you know that your labor is not in vain."

(1 Cor. 15:58 NIV) "And let us not grow weary while doing good, for in due season we shall reap if we do not lose heart." (Gal. 6:9) Striving to please God in your walk with Him produces the best that you have to offer in everything that you do. Not only does God reward you, but others take notice of you, too. You don't have to be *the* best, just be *your best*, trusting God to do the rest.

I AM HIGHLY ESTEEMED BY BOTH GOD AND MAN

"And so find favor and **high esteem in the sight of God and man."** *-Proverbs 3:4*

Proverbs 10:7 says, "The memory of the righteous is blessed, but the name of the wicked will rot." Your character is who you are. Your reputation is who people think you are. I had a bad reputation, and rightly so. I did a lot of bad things. People would say, "You're this. You're that." I would respond by telling them, "That's what I do. That's not who I am." Nobody ever understood that. There are probably still people that think I'm still the same, that I could never be anything but what they've always known me to be. I don't let that discourage me. God says that I'm righteous (1 Jn. 3:7) and because of that I have high esteem *with Him and with man*. It takes time to build a reputation. It takes diligence in doing right and being right, in order to build a good reputation. It only takes a moment to destroy it. God gives you high esteem, but you have to keep it. If you place a high priority on building your character into that of a godly person, your reputation will conform to that. You're not just thrown out there on your own. The Holy Spirit lives within you to help you. He will convict you, guide you, lead others to help you, and keep others away from you that could potentially harm or hinder you. Making a good name for yourself is God's business. It really shouldn't be your concern what other people think of you. The only one you have to please is the Lord. When you strive for that, everything right and good falls into place. (Mt. 6:33) Another point I want to make here is the importance of the company you keep. You can be a born again, Holy Ghost filled, water walking, light bearing Christian living a victorious, fruitful life, but if the people you hang out with are known for their foul language, excessive partying, sleeping around, lying, and stealing, it rubs off on you. We are to be light to those people, but we don't go to the bar with them or get involved in their activities. (Amos 3:3) Love the sinner, but hate the sin. That's why Jesus sent the disciples out 2 by 2, for accountability. You are not your past and don't believe anyone who tries to convince you otherwise. Believe God. You are His. You are called by His Name. You are His child, one of His people. That is your new reputation.

I TRUST IN THE LORD WITH ALL MY HEART

"Trust in the Lord with all your heart and lean not on your own understanding;" Proverbs 3:5

Something that kept me from coming to the Lord sooner than I did was my inability to logically explain or understand things in the Bible. I couldn't wrap my mind around how things happened, therefore, I didn't believe they were true. Well, thank God for being God, because if this world alone, much less the universe, were put together by my limited understanding, we would all be in a mess. I "somehow" (thank You, Holy Spirit) knew this was a stumbling block for me, so one day I decided, no matter what the Bible said, I was going to believe it. I literally thought to myself, "If the Bible says pink elephants can fly, I'm going to start looking for them in the sky." I made the choice to trust God *according to His Word*. Each time, He was faithful. That enabled me to trust Him more and for bigger things. He built my trust in Him, not the other way around. The only part I had in it was making the choice to trust and believe. Now, I trust Him in all things. His track record is perfect. Things rarely happen in the way or timing that I expect, but they do happen, and most often, His promises are fulfilled abundantly above anything I could ask or think. You don't have to figure it out. Simply yield to God. Martin Luther King, Jr. said, "Faith is taking the first step even when you don't see the whole staircase." God cannot lie. (Num. 23:19) He *is* Truth. (Jn. 16:13) When you go to the drive-thru at a fast food restaurant, you order your food, then go to a window and pay for it, then you drive up to another window to get your food. You are driving up to that next window in faith, believing that you are about to get some food. Faith is that simple. You find a promise from the Bible that applies to you, you take it to God in prayer, you speak that Word, believing that God will do it or that He's already done it, and you receive it. (Mk. 11:23-24) Just like at the drive-thru, you may have to pull over and park while that promise is being made ready, but when it comes, it will be fresh, and often times, there will be an extra order of fries or a drink because you had to wait.

I DO NOT LEAN ON MY OWN UNDERSTANDING

*"Trust in the Lord with all your heart and **lean not on your own understanding;"** Proverbs 3:5*

I am the first person to admit that my understanding of things is often scrambled, yet I always think I have to know the how and why of everything before I can fully commit. I've come to accept that I think differently than other people. I'm wired different. I struggled with that most of my life, but accepting it for what it is has given me freedom to move forward. It's okay to not have all the answers. It's okay to ask questions. It's even okay to thoroughly research everything in every way imaginable. In Acts chapter 8, the Ethiopian eunuch in charge of the queen's treasury was riding in his chariot reading Isaiah. The Angel of the Lord had told Philip to go to him, and when he saw the eunuch, Philip asked him if he understood what he was reading. The eunuch asked Philip, "How can I, unless someone guides me?" Then, in verse 34 he asks Philip who the Scripture was referring to. In Acts chapter 17, Paul and Silas were sent to Berea. The people there were receptive to their message, but the Bible says they "searched the Scriptures daily to find out whether these things were so". They checked Paul and Silas' teaching against the Word. None of that makes you stupid. In fact, it's the Biblically correct, intelligent thing to do. Whenever something is beyond your understanding, pray first and ask God to give you wisdom. (Jms. 1:5) Speak to people in your church. Research online. But... always check whatever you find to see if it lines up with God's Word. "For a time is coming when people will no longer listen to right teaching. They will follow their own desires and will look for teachers who will tell them whatever they want to hear. (2 Tim. 4:3 NIV) Just like with doctors, you can shop around until you find one that gives you what you want or tells you to do what others have told you not to do, but Truth is infallible and unchanging. You don't have to understand everything perfectly, but you do have to stick to the Truth. If you sincerely seek to understand a thing, God will reveal it to you. Until you do understand it, you can trust God along the way, knowing that He is in control and that He loves you.

I ACKNOWLEDGE GOD IN ALL MY WAYS

"In all your ways acknowledge Him and He shall direct your paths." Proverbs 3:6

The first thing I want to point out is that all means all, not some or most, but *all*. Acknowledging God in all things takes time. It takes practice. It is immensely worth the effort it takes to learn it. My immediate thought on "acknowledge" was to recognize or affirm. The Hebrew meaning, though, says "acknowledge" means to "know, understand, consider, declare, respect". The best way to know someone is to spend time with them, to listen to them. So, you start with the Bible. Along the way, you pray. Ask God what things mean. I don't mean to read your Bible a few days and then go off in some other direction. Spend time with God every day, reading His Word and staying in constant communication with God regarding everything, in addition to regular prayer time. Think on what you've read as you go through your day. Be open to doing things in a new way. When you humble yourself and submit to God's ways, He will lead you. The things you didn't know you could or should do will become clear to you. You will likely have to step out of your comfort zone. This is where you trust and believe. And this is where He is glorified. God gets the glory for the good things He does in your life. Your victory is solidly guaranteed. You will still have days that go bad and people that don't like you and things go wrong, but you will have peace, a better life, joy, favor, eternal life, purpose, and you will have God. My best day before I fully submitted to God doesn't compare to my worst day since. I used to have panic attacks over the smallest things. I never knew what to do or how to do it. I know now that by acknowledging God through His Word and prayer, He is going to lead me in the right way, even if it doesn't make sense to me at the time. He is never going to make me look or feel bad because that would make Him look bad. God is on your side to give you abundant life. (Jn. 10:10) A life of victory gives God glory. Another important part of acknowledging God is agreeing with Him. If the Bible says it, believe it. Don't ever say, "Not me." When you do that, you're agreeing with the devil. You *are* above and not beneath, the head and not the tail, an overcomer. Include God in *everything* you think, say, and do.

GOD DIRECTS MY PATHS

*"In all your ways acknowledge Him and **He shall direct your paths.**" Proverbs 3:6*

When you involve God in everything you do, you don't have to worry about the how's and who's and when's. God will make all things work together for your good. (Rom. 8:28) People you don't even know will cross your path at exactly the right time to do exactly what needs to be done. God makes a way out of no way. (Is. 43:16) That's what He does! You won't necessarily hear Him audibly, but you may, saying, "This is the way. Walk in it." (Is. 30:21) He will just line things up to lead you in the direction He wants you to go. There's an old song called "He's An On-Time God". Sometimes God shows up at what seems like the last moment before all hell breaks loose. But He does show up, and when He does, He shows out. Sometimes it's a test of our faith. Sometimes it's His mercy and grace. Mankind is severely lacking in ability and reliability. God is not limited by anything in any way. God is completely trustworthy. The Creator of all things gave you life. (Gen. 2:7) Give it back to Him, to do with as He originally purposed. (Jer. 29:11) By doing so, you will find yourself really alive like never before. At 55 years old, I am more alive than I've ever been. Before, I had a pulse and that was about it. I had no purpose, no direction. I was living in spiritual darkness, which is spiritual death, and I didn't even know it until I was made alive in Christ. (Eph. 2:1-5) Since then, God has directed my paths into beautiful places that I never would have expected or imagined, and He still is. I don't even want to try to maneuver my way through life on my own. I need God and so do you. Being a "bench-warmer" Christian isn't good enough. Engage. Lean on God for absolutely everything. He's your Lord, your Helper, your Father, your Physician, your Creator, and the Captain of your soul. Get out of the way and let Him navigate.

I AM NOT WISE IN MY OWN EYES

"Do not be wise in your own eyes; fear the Lord and depart from evil." Proverbs 3:7

Oh boy! Does that say, "I am not wise in my own eyes *anymore*?" I thought I knew everything and if I didn't know something, nobody did. I've learned that the more I think I know, the less I really do know. Like I've said, I am at the point, praise the Lord, where I don't have to have all the answers. (Or think I do.) Nobody does. The best position you can be in is that of depending on God. The first step to surrender is giving it all, *all*, to God and leaving it there. If God shows you something in the Spirit, you can bank on it. Sometimes He will lead you to someone or a message or His Word, but until and unless that happens, you can only assume to know the entirety of a situation. And that is totally okay. To fear the Lord means to respect Him and be in awe of Him, to know that He isn't like man. He is God Almighty, and there is no other. His Word is eternal. God put His Spirit in us for many reasons, one of which is to guide us in living according to His ways. His ways are found in His Word, but what if there isn't a specific Scripture regarding certain things. For instance, there aren't specific Scriptures saying don't use drugs, but the Scriptures do speak of sorcery and witchcraft, which in Greek is the word "pharmakeia". That's where the word "pharmacy" comes from. The literal translation of the Greek word is "a drug, spell giving potion; enchantment with drugs". Sorcery and witchcraft are clearly forbidden throughout the Bible. (Lev. 19:26) You may have to dig deep, but God says, "How can a young man cleanse his way? By taking heed according to Your Word." (Ps. 119:9) Some of the best adventures I've been on were when God took me on a journey through His Word, studying the Hebrew and Greek meanings, praying, and being led all over the Bible, being blessed with revelation of Scriptures. I've spent entire days with God in His Word on adventures like that. I suggest you try it. It will blow you away! Being wise in your own eyes is pride. In Job 38:4-7, God asks Job, "Where were you when I laid the foundations of the earth? Who determined it's measurements? Who put boundaries around the sea?" It wasn't Job, and neither was it you or me, or anybody, but God alone. Not having all the answers doesn't mean you aren't intelligent. The smartest thing you will ever do is surrender to and trust the One who does have all the answers.

I FEAR THE LORD

*"Do not be wise in your own eyes; **fear the Lord** and depart from evil." Proverbs 3:7*

Revelation 14:7 says, "Fear God and give glory to Him, for the hour of His judgment has come; and worship Him who made Heaven and earth, the sea and springs of water." This is good embodiment of what it means to fear the Lord. A lot of people see God as a big, mean God, waiting to punish and send everybody to hell. That's what I used to think, too. I knew I couldn't measure up against the most lenient standards, much less all the laws and commandments. Because of what Christ accomplished on the Cross and through His resurrection, I don't have to. It isn't about being perfect and sinless. It's about love and forgiveness. People tend to see God the way they experienced their fathers. Some people had absent fathers. Some had abusive fathers. Some had emotionally distant fathers. That's how they view God. Even those people that had good fathers can have a distorted image of God based on their fathers, because no father is perfect *except* God. To fear God doesn't mean to be scared of Him or that He's mean or He's going to abandon you if you mess up. It means to live according to His terms out of love and respect and wanting to please Him. It means giving Him credit for every good thing in your life. It means that if you do mess up, you're still loved because He loves *you* no matter what, and no less than if you hadn't messed up. You will still have consequences for your actions, because God corrects *those He loves*. (Prov. 3:12) To fear the Lord also means to worship Him regularly. I know a lady in her late 50s whose daddy is in his 80s. She still talks about him like she's a little girl. She's always talking about him like he's the best thing since Twinkies. How you worship is between you and God. He does say to worship Him with song and dance, but for me personally, I worship Him through serving Him in the ministry, through the time I spend in His Word and prayer and being the hands and feet and voice of Jesus. I worship by sacrificing my old ways to conform to His ways, so that I can be just like my Daddy when I grow up!

I DEPART FROM EVIL

*"Do not be wise in your own eyes; fear the Lord and **depart from evil.**" Proverbs 3:7*

It's easy to walk away from certain types of evil, those which are overtly and obviously evil. Others are sometimes walked away from because the person doesn't want to get involved. How often do you walk away from gossip, complaining, self-centeredness, greed, narcissism, vanity, and other such "minor" forms of evil? Evil is evil, period. Just like sin is sin. Evil exists in this world. God even allows evil, but He can turn it around for good. Mankind is responsible for their part in evil. Therefore, it's your responsibility to turn from evil. God will help you to do that. I tried for many, many years to depart from drug addiction, which comes with all sorts of evil attached to it. The harder I tried on my own to quit, the worse things got for me. I was in a drug house one night and the dealer fell asleep. I knew better than to get up and walk around, lest anything come up missing and I get blamed. The only thing within my reach, other than my own possessions, was a Bible. It was open to Hosea and I read the first thing my eyes landed on, Hosea 14:4. "I will heal their backsliding. I will love them freely." I had been born again at that time, but was in a severely backslidden state. The Holy Spirit lived in me, but I had started using drugs again and stopped going to church. I knew enough to take that Scripture and stand on it, no matter what my life looked like, no matter how long it took. To me, that Scripture said, "GOD will heal my backsliding. Not me. GOD." So I believed Him. And in time, His timing, He did. It was nothing at all that I did. And when He did, it was just the beginning of deliverance from all kinds of evil. It didn't happen overnight and it didn't happen all at one time, but it happened and it's still happening. God can take away every form of evil in your life all at once, but He usually does it little by little so that you will grow and learn through the process, and so that you won't think it was *you* who did it. (Deut. 7:22) God wants *all* the glory for your life and He deserves it. Even if it looks like it was you who did these amazing things, it was God who made it possible, it was God who put it on your heart to have the desire to change, and God who *keeps you changed and brings you back*, even when you fail miserably like I did. To fear the Lord is wisdom, and to depart from evil is understanding. (Job 28:28) Don't give up. God *wants* to help you add this to your testimony.

I HONOR GOD WITH MY POSSESSIONS

"Honor the Lord with your possessions; and with the firstfruits of all your increase." Proverbs 3:9

This is an easy thing to explain, but it can be a hard thing to do sometimes. When God blesses you with something, make sure to use it for His glory. For instance, let's say God blesses you with a new cell phone. How you use that phone honors or dishonors Him. If you get on the phone and call your friends, or they call you, and the conversation revolves around bad mouthing that mom in the pick up line at school that wears low cut shirts, or you tell what you heard about so and so's husband and his affairs, or if you use the phone to watch pornography or indulge in online drama, that's dishonoring God. I'm not saying that everything you do with the phone has to be pious and holy, but certainly it shouldn't be any form of immoral or sinful behavior. I used to play non-violent video games sometimes, but it became an idol, so I took them off my phone. . I stay in touch with people, but none of my old drug buddies. None. I mainly use my phone to locate Scriptures, read articles and sermons, things that not only glorify God, but pertain to Him, because that's my main focus. I want you to realize that every good thing you have is from God. ((Jms. 1:17) Another way to honor God is to use what He's given you to bless others. My friend was blessed with an SUV, so she decided to use it to bless others who didn't have transportation. God also gave her the gift of being able to do hair, and she blesses women by doing their hair. She never charges people for anything, and when she can, she pays for everything herself. In fact, she lives a life of blessing and she's been a tremendous influence on me in many ways. I want you to read Matthew 25:35-40. Whatever you have, do your best to bless others with it, expecting nothing in return. You may not have money, you may have time, or a special gift, or special wisdom. Whatever it is, ask God how you can bless others with what He's given you. That's what the Kingdom of God is all about. That brings honor and glory to the Father. It brings thanks to God. In being the literal hands, feet, and heart of Jesus to a lost and hurting world, you are the carrier of love and compassion, which is from God.

I HONOR GOD WITH THE FIRSTFRUITS OF ALL MY INCREASE

*"**Honor the Lord** with your possessions; and **with the firstfruits of all your increase.**" Proverbs 3:9*

A lot of people confuse firstfruits with tithes, but they are different. The tithe is the first 10 percent of all your increase and it's a commandment. (Mal. 3:10) The tithe is given throughout the year, each time you receive increase of any kind, whether it be money or goods. The firstfruits is a free will offering. Originally, the firstfruits offering referred to the first harvest of the new season. There was no specific amount required, but it was important because what the person gave was in proportion to their faith that God would bless their remaining crops. Most people these days aren't full time farmers, so what exactly does firstfruits look like in this day and age? Firstfruits are any income, wealth, or goods that you are blessed with over the course of the year. It is normally given once a year. A good example is tax time. A lot of people receive a refund in excess of their normal amount of income. This would be a good time to give a firstfruit offering. The amount is entirely up to you, but keep in mind that the more you trust God to bless you in the remainder of the year, the more you should give to reflect that trust. I also have a belief in using time in regard to tithing and firstfruit offerings. I know that if I give the first part of my day to the Lord, He blesses me for honoring Him. When I go beyond that, spending more time with Him throughout the day than I normally do, He never ever disappoints me. His presence surrounds me, I hear from Him clearly and often, I am filled with joy, and He protects me and blesses my socks off left and right. God sees everything and knows everything. He knows the condition of your heart- why you do things. God loves a cheerful giver (2 Cor. 9:7) He also loves a heart full of gratitude. It can be confusing sometimes, but just remember 1 Corinthians 10:31 and you'll do great, "Therefore, whether you eat or drink, or *whatever you do*, do all to the glory of God."

I HAVE FOUND LIFE

*"For whoever finds Me **finds life**, and obtains favor from the Lord;"*
Proverbs 8:35

This Scripture is speaking about Wisdom. In Proverbs 8:22-23 Wisdom says, "The Lord possessed Me at the beginning of His way, before His works of old. I have been established from everlasting, from the beginning, before there was ever an earth." Wisdom is the Word of God. Jesus Christ is the Living Word. (Jn. 1:1) Jesus came so that you may have abundant life. (Jn. 10:10) Jesus said in John 14:6, "I am the Way, the Truth, and the Life". Whoever finds Jesus finds life. The Bible says that "Wisdom is the principal thing; therefore get wisdom. And in all your getting, get understanding." (Prov. 4:7) Wisdom brings abundant life, and you can't have fullness of life without Christ. Until I was born again, I lived in a blur. I did it on purpose. Life was too much for me to handle. Even when I could manage short periods of functionality, I was so blind to what really living meant. It may have looked like I had gotten myself together here and there, but the eyes of my heart were completely blinded. I lived in the flesh and had no idea what living in the Spirit was. I was totally self-absorbed. My life revolved around addiction. When you open your Bible, God opens your spiritual eyes. When you open your mouth to speak the Word, God opens doors that no man can close and closes doors that no man can open. (Rev. 3:7-8) The Word of God, the Wisdom of God, gave me new life. I'm no longer the living dead. I have purpose. I love myself. I am able to love others. I know and love God. I have *experienced* Jesus Christ. I've been rescued from every form of evil. I have eternal life. I no longer am waiting for my life to be over. It's just beginning, and when I do move on, it will be to spend eternity in the presence of God and with my loved ones. "Awake, awake, O Zion, clothe yourself with strength. Put on your garments of splendor, O Jerusalem, the holy city. The uncircumcised and defiled will not enter you again. Shake off your dust; rise up, sit enthroned, O Jerusalem. Free yourself from the chains on your neck, O captive Daughter of Zion." (Is. 52:1-2 NIV) Your deliverance is already there. Walk into newness of life, fullness of life. The wisdom of the Word is your roadmap.

I AM FAVORED

*"For whoever finds me finds life, and **obtains favor from the Lord;"***
Proverbs 8:35

Wisdom and knowledge are often thought to be the same thing, but they are not. Knowledge is knowing something. Wisdom is using that knowledge, applying it to a specific situation. Biblical wisdom is pure. (Jms. 3:17) Biblical wisdom is truth because the Word of God is Truth. The Holy Spirit is called the Spirit of Truth. (Jn. 16:13) So, the Spirit of Wisdom is a part of the Holy Spirit. (Is. 11:2) When you seek out wisdom from the Word, it's up to you to apply it to your situation, but the Holy Spirit will help you. "If any of you lacks wisdom, let him ask of God, who gives to all liberally and without reproach, *and it will be given to him*." (Jms. 1:5) True wisdom can't be found in the things of the world. It's found only in the things of God. "My son, if you receive My Words, and treasure My commands within you, tune your ears to wisdom, and concentrate on understanding. Cry out for insight and understanding. Search for them as you would for lost money or hidden treasure. Then you will understand what it means to fear the Lord, and you will gain knowledge of God. For the Lord grants wisdom! From His mouth come knowledge and understanding. He grants a treasure of good sense to the godly. He is their shield, protecting those who walk with integrity." (Prov. 2:1-7 NIV) This is God's promise to you that He will cover you when you seek out His ways and follow them. Wisdom from God results in righteousness. Psalm 5:12 says, "For You, O Lord, will bless the righteous; *with favor You will surround him as with a shield.*" Following the ways of Truth enables you to walk in favor in every circumstance, everywhere you go, by the power of the Holy Spirit. Favor includes blessings, healing, protection, provision, revelation, peace, and joy. God will open doors that no man can close and close doors that no man can open. (Rev. 3:7) "The steps of a good man are ordered by the Lord, and he delights in his way." (Ps. 37:23) See, the Lord delights in you when you delight in Him. Supernatural divine favor surrounds you when you apply the Word to your life.

I AM WORTHY

*"Who can find a virtuous wife? For **her worth is far above rubies.**"*
Proverbs 31:10

There is nothing that you've ever done, nothing that anyone else has done to you or said about you, nothing in all your life that you've experienced, that diminishes God's love for you. You were created in His image. You are valuable to God and you always have been. You are a special treasure to God. (1 Ptr. 2:9) God is all-knowing. (1 Jn. 3:20) He knows the end from the beginning. (Is. 46:10) Nothing in your life surprises Him, and He still says you are worthy. Jesus died for you, *while you were still a sinner*. (Rom. 5:8) It's so important to know without a shadow of a doubt who God says you are, because anything that doesn't agree with that is a lie. I was fed those lies my whole life. I believed those lies. When I started finding out about who God says I am, it dawned on me that everything else was lies, lies, lies, even the things I thought about myself. The devil is a liar. (Jn. 8:44) God's Word is Truth (Jn. 17:17) and He cannot lie. (Titus 1:2) Every Word of God's Truth says that you are worthy, you are valuable, you are loved, you are precious. "For I know the thoughts that I think toward you, says the Lord, thoughts of peace and not of evil, to give you a future and a hope." (Jer. 29:11) God wants you to live an abundant life. (Jn. 10:10) The devil doesn't want you to know the Truth about who God says you are because then he has no control over you. All he can do then is try to tempt you. When you are walking according to God's ways, speaking God's Words in the face of temptation and trials, the devil is completely shut down. That's what Jesus did. (Mt. 4:1-11) The devil doesn't attack anything that isn't valuable. You are God's workmanship, created in Christ Jesus for good works, which God prepared beforehand that you should walk in them. (Eph. 2:10) You are valuable to God, His inheritance. (Eph. 1:18) You are of great substance. You are a child of God, therefore you are worthy. (Deut. 7:6-8)

I AM GOD FEARING

*"Charm is deceitful and beauty is passing, but a woman **who fears the Lord**, she shall be praised." Proverbs 31:30*

To fear God doesn't mean to be afraid of Him. It means that you have such awe and respect for Him that you put Him first in *all* things and that you obey His Word. God is love. There is no fear in love, but perfect love casts out fear. (1 Jn. 4:8) When you are God fearing, you will be misunderstood by unbelievers. You may even be socially outcast. To be God fearing means that you stand firm in these circumstances, because you fear God more than you fear man. God will honor you because doing that honors Him. I had a friend that was born again, but she still had an outstanding criminal charge that hadn't been resolved. She turned herself into the police, and at first she was okay because there were other women where she was that were seeking God, but then she was moved to a different dorm, and nobody there had the least bit of interest in hearing about God, much less having Bible studies. She became very depressed. My advice to her was to keep trying, because at the first bit of trouble, the most hardened inmate would come running to *her* for help, and that's exactly what happened. Matthew 10:26-28 says, "Therefore do not fear them. For there is nothing covered that will not be revealed, and hidden that will not be known. Whatever I tell you in the dark, speak in the light; and what you hear in the ear, preach on the housetops. And do not fear those who kill the body but cannot kill the soul. But rather fear Him who is able to destroy both soul and body in hell." Jesus calls you to be a sheep in the midst of wolves. (Mt. 10:16) In the same verse, He says to be "wise as serpents and harmless as doves." As a Christian, you are to be in the world, but not of the world. (Jn. 17:14) That's where your light shines brightest, in darkness. You are called to be a light. Burn as brightly as you can.

I AM PRAISED

*"Charm is deceitful and beauty is passing, but a woman who fears the Lord, she **shall be praised.**" Proverbs 31:30*

What is your most praise-worthy quality? Your job, your house, your looks? All those things can be taken away in an instant. Fear of the Lord results in righteousness, integrity, compassion, love. The way you live your life speaks to others. When your life reflects fear of the Lord, a commitment to his ways, you are praised, even if you never hear a word of it.. "When a man's ways please the Lord, He makes even His enemies to be at peace with him." (Prov. 16:7) Have you ever known anyone that tries desperately to still look like a 20-something, even though they're well past 40? Or seen a very pretty woman that uses profanity every other word? Or a man that thinks he has to prove how manly he is? It counteracts the thing they seek to accomplish. Being a God-fearing person displays Christ-like qualities- humility, generosity, joy, patience, peace. People want those things, if not in themselves, they still want those things in others. You can't buy them, you can't borrow them. They come from God. The fruit of the Holy Spirit is love, joy, peace, patience, kindness, goodness, faithfulness, gentleness, and self control. (Gal. 5:22-23) These are praise-worthy qualities, no matter who you are. These qualities don't go away. They endure, sometimes even long after a person is gone. Being a solid, dependable, trustworthy person of integrity is a gift to others. Sharing God's love is a gift to others. There will always be people that talk about you, no matter how much good you do. Be the person that, when they do, other people will defend you, praising the God in you.

I AM KEPT BUSY WITH THE JOY OF MY HEART

*"For He will not dwell unduly on the days of his life, because **God keeps him busy with the joy of his heart.**" Ecclesiastes 5:20*

Everything that you have is from God. He delights to bless you. As you acknowledge His blessings, both great and small, let go of the past. Those things, those circumstances, are gone. God has moved you into a new place. 2 Corinthians 5:17 says, "Therefore, if anyone is in Christ, he is a new creation; old things have passed away; behold, all things have become new." The past has passed away. It's dead. It's time to bury it. You can't live in the fullness of joy that God intends for you if you keep digging up the dead body of your past. And you certainly can't drag the dead body of the past around. It will wear you out. You already know this. Bury the past. "Therefore, if the Son makes you free, you will be free indeed." (Jn. 8:36) An exercise I like to do is to literally count my blessings. I start thinking of blessings, naming them, and thanking God. I thank God for every single thing I can think of, my bed, a place to live, even good soap and shampoo, because I remember not having them. I thank Him for healthy food to eat, because I remember having to eat whatever I could get, not what was good for me. I thank God for delivering me from drugs, abuse, being locked up, cigarettes, depression, death. I thank Him for rescuing my life, from myself, from illness, from toxic relationships. I thank God for the people in my life. I thank God for my health and clean clothes and air conditioning and heat. The list is endless. I have peace now. I used to be such an angry, hateful person. I cried all the time. I cry tears of joy now. God Himself is the joy of my heart. "But seek first the Kingdom of God and His righteousness, and all these things shall be added to you." (Mt. 6:33) "Trust in the Lord, and do good; dwell in the land, and feed on his faithfulness. Delight yourself also in the Lord, and He shall give you the desires of your heart." (Ps. 37:3-4)

I AM WILLING AND OBEDIENT

*"If **you are willing and obedient**, you shall eat the good of the land." Isaiah 1:19*

God's Word is His instruction manual for your life. He wants you to *want* to use it, rather than feel it's a duty. God loves you and wants only good for you. That doesn't mean that bad things won't happen, but that when they do, if you will follow the instructions, you will be better than you were without them, and you will grow and mature in the process. God is always with you. Nothing will ever change that. If you and I spent the day together and neither of us talked, we probably wouldn't want to spend another day like that, right? It's the same with God, except that He would still want to spend another day with you, hoping that the next day you would talk to Him. And He does that again and again and again. Charles Spurgeon said, "When I pray, I talk to God, but when I read the Bible, God talks to me." When God speaks through His Word, it's to lead you and guide you into becoming the person He created you to be. Obedience is vital to that life. In my life, I've never had structure or self-discipline, until being born again. The desire to do so did not come naturally. It was a product of the Holy Spirit working inside me. (Gal. 5:22-23) Because I love God and want to conform to the image of Christ, I submit myself to Him, to have His way with me, in all that concerns me. I've failed many times, but I've learned and grown through those failures. I am not the same person I was a year ago, and that person isn't the same person that I was 2 years ago. It takes time. But God has abundantly blessed me every step of the way, even when I failed. Spiritual growth is priceless. So is a close, personal relationship with God. Spending time with God will result in your desire to be obedient to Him. He's your Father and the closer you get to Him, the more you will desire the things He desires. And like any good Father, He wants to lavish His love on you. He wants to give you the best that He has, and He owns *everything*, including things that money can't buy. Your obedience will bring great rewards.

I EAT THE GOOD OF THE LAND

*"If you are willing and obedient, **you shall eat the good of the land."** Isaiah 1:19*

The good of the land refers to God's provision for you. God provides supernaturally. That means that you may not be able to comprehend how it will happen, but you can rest in knowing that if He said He would, He will. But... notice the beginning of this verse says "IF you are WILLING and OBEDIENT". A few years ago, I started going to a church near where I lived. I really liked it, so I kept going back. I was diabetic, and didn't have money to buy healthy food. I found out after I had been going a few weeks that this church had a food pantry one day a week for the public, and every time a person went to service there, they could go to the pantry, too. I was amazed at the size and selection of this food pantry. And they had everything I needed to keep my sugar levels low. There's no coincidence with God. He arranges everything. Now, I'm literally talking about food, but God will always make a way where there seems to be no way (Is. 43:16) and not just with food. God's provision covers all your physical, emotional, spiritual, and financial needs. Whatever need you have, God is in control of it. That doesn't mean you can use God like an ATM machine. Psalm 37:4 says, "Delight yourself in the Lord, and He will give you the desires of your heart." God gave me revelation on this Scripture. Where it says that He gives you the desires of your heart, it doesn't mean that He gives you anything you want. It means that He places those desires inside of you. Then, when you ask Him for those things, He most certainly will give them to you. He's just waiting for you to ask Him. But it has to be in His will for you. God is all-knowing, so He knows what's good for you and what isn't. You have to trust Him, but He will give you so much more than you actually need. Another thing that God has changed in me is my level of contentment. I am content with so much less materially, even though nothing I've ever had compares to the spiritual things God has given me. You will not only eat the good of the land, you will dwell in that land, by your willingness to surrender to Jesus and your obedience to His Word.

I DO NOT FEAR

*"But now, thus says the Lord, who created you, O Jacob, and He who formed you, O Israel; "**Fear not**, for I have redeemed you; I have called you by name. you are Mine.""* Isaiah 43:1

The Bible says "Fear not" 365 times. That's once for each day of the year. When God repeats something even once, it's because He wants you to *get it*. So 365 times means He *really* means it. Fear is more than an emotion. It's a demonic spirit. God clearly says that He did not give you a spirit of fear, but of power, and of love, and of a sound mind. (2 Tim. 1:7) If the spirit of fear is not from God, it can only be from one other place- the devil. The spirit of fear torments. It opens the door for other evil spirits to enter. I was paralyzed by fear most of my life. I couldn't say or do the simplest of things. I was critically shy and easily embarrassed. I had anxiety and panic attacks. There were several times in my life, starting when I was a teenager, that I refused to leave the house for extended periods. When I became an adult, I stayed indoors for over a year. Twice. Normal fear is a natural response to danger, but demonic fear is extreme. It manifests itself in many ways. Hoarding is a form of fear. Isolation is a form of fear. Anxiety, timidity, procrastination, those are all forms of fear. Jesus came to set the captives free. (Is. 61:1) He came to set free all who were bound by any spirit that is not from

God. The devil attacks the mind. He uses *your own voice* to speak lies to you, and because what you hear is in your voice, you think it's your own thought. One way to know for sure that it isn't your own thought, is the devil will bombard you to the point that you think you can't shut the voice up. Another way to know is when you wonder, "Where did *that* come from?" When the devil tried to tempt Jesus, Jesus fought back with the Word of God. Every temptation was counteracted with, "It is written…" (Mt. 4:4-7) The key to shutting fear down is to recognize it immediately and cast it down. Any negative or tormenting thought can be cast down by speaking out loud, "I cast down every argument and high thing that exalts itself against the knowledge of God. I bring every thought captive to the obedience of Jesus Christ. In the Name of Jesus." (2 Cor. 10:4-5) When I was coming off drugs, I did this. At first, I said this many, many times throughout the day, and even in the middle of the night. Over time, I didn't have to say it as much, because I was no longer tormented by thoughts of using drugs. Trust God to deliver you from fear.

I AM REDEEMED

*"But now, thus says the Lord, who created you, O Jacob, and He who formed you, O Israel; "Fear not, for **I have redeemed you**; I have called you by your name; you are Mine."" Isaiah 43:1*

To redeem means to purchase. In ancient Jewish culture, to redeem someone was a duty for the next of kin to fulfill to their dead relative. When a man died, the next of kin was responsible for buying the man's property, to keep it within the family. This included the deceased man's wife. She then became the kinsman's wife. Because of the fall of man in the Garden of Eden, we were returned to the kingdom of darkness. When Christ shed His Blood on the Cross, He paid the price to buy every one of us back. As soon as you received Jesus as your Lord and Savior, you became His property, but you are so much more to Him. He loves you, and that wasn't necessarily part of the deal in ancient times. Christ is different. His love cost Him His life. He suffered, so that you don't have to. He died, so that you would have eternal life with Him. His death proved that He was human, but His resurrection proved that He was God. Everything He ever did was out of love. John 10:29 says, "My Father, who has given them to Me, is greater than *all*; and *no one* is able to snatch them out of My Father's hand." You now belong to Jesus and that will never, ever change, no matter what you do, no matter what anyone says, no matter how you feel. That's the truth of God's own Word. "For you were bought at a price; therefore glorify God in your body and in your spirit, which are God's." (1 Cor. 6:20) You are redeemed from every form of ungodliness and worldly lust, that you should live soberly, righteously, and godly, that Christ might redeem you from every lawless deed and purify you for Himself as His own special people, for doing good works. (Titus 2:11-14) Speak this confession often, because it declares

Whose you are, as well as who you are. Psalm 107:2 says, "Let the redeemed of the Lord say so, whom He has redeemed from the hand of the adversary." Shout it in the devil's face!

GOD CALLED ME BY MY NAME

*"But now, thus says the Lord, who created you , O Jacob, and He who formed you, O Israel; "Fear not, for I have redeemed you; **I have called you by your name**; you are Mine.""* Isaiah 43:1

When someone calls you by your name, it means they know you. Most likely, you didn't know God when He called you by your name, but He knew you. "Before I formed you in the womb, I knew you." (Jer 1:3) Even the hairs of your head are counted. (Mt. 10:30) He knows when you sit down and when you stand, He knows all your ways, He knows your thoughts before you think them. He knows everywhere you go. He formed you in the womb and His eyes saw you before you were even formed. His thoughts toward you are precious, and are too numerous to count. (Ps. 139) "When I consider Your Heavens, the work of Your fingers, the moon and the stars, which You have ordained, what is man that You are mindful of him, and the son of man that You visit him?" (Ps. 8:3-4) God didn't call your name by accident. You are His beloved child and He wants you to know that, without any doubt. You were chosen by Him, to be His love child, His holy people, to do good in His Name. He rescued you from a life of sin and death to live an abundant life, both now and in eternity. God knows you personally, better than you even know yourself. His desire for you is goodness and peace. ""For I know the thoughts that I think toward you," says the Lord, "thoughts of peace and not of evil, to give you a future and a hope. Then you will call upon Me and go and pray to Me, and I will listen to you. And you will seek Me and find Me, when you search for Me with all your heart."" (Jer. 29:11-13) Names were important during Biblical times. They foretold of a person's destiny. In a world filled with titles and labels, your name is very personal. It sets you apart and distinguishes you from others. Calling you by name indicates a relationship. That is God's full intention. He doesn't just want you to hear about Him or read about Him, He wants a relationship with you, a loving relationship, as that of a Father and His child. His love for you is tender and intimate. Of all the people that have ever lived, He chose you and called *you* by your name.

I BELONG TO GOD

*"But now, thus says the Lord, who created you, O Jacob, and He who formed you, O Israel; "Fear not, for I have redeemed you; I have called you by your name; **you are Mine**.""* Isaiah 43:1

For anyone who has ever felt like an outsider, a misfit, like they didn't fit in or weren't accepted, this is a beautiful thing. God not only accepts you, He accepts you just as you are. You don't have to try to be good enough or smart enough or rich enough. You don't have to "get fixed" first, either. God is the ultimate Creator and Artist. He specializes in making beautiful, mosaic masterpieces out of shattered lives. The belief that you have to "get right" before you get with God is one of the biggest lies the devil ever told, and a lot of people believe it. I did. I used to think that I couldn't approach God until I got off drugs, or everything about my life was perfect. If that's what you're waiting for, you'll *never* get there because without God, you can't get deep soul healing, not in a way that your healing is whole and complete. The truth is, that's when you need God the most. To belong to God means that you are in a loving relationship with Him. His love for you isn't based on anything you do. It's *who He is*. Belonging to God means that resurrection power is available to you, so that your life can truly be transformed. You will never be alone. The Spirit of God lives inside of you. All you have to do is trust and believe. You are spiritually connected to Almighty God. That's an unbreakable bond. For the first time in your life, you will know acceptance like never before because *you were created for acceptance in the Beloved.* (Eph. 1:6) No other acceptance fulfills this longing because no other acceptance is acceptable. Only God can fulfill this need. Belonging to God also means that He protects you, provides for you, favors you, guides you. You can claim *all* the promises of God with confidence and boldness. You are a part of God's eternal family, *now.* Belonging to God also means that you are called to live differently. "I have been crucified with Christ; it is no longer I who live, but Christ lives in me; and *the life which I now live in the flesh I live by faith in the Son of God,* who loved me and gave Himself for me." (Gal. 2:20) "For you were bought at a price; therefore glorify God in your body and in your spirit, which are God's." (1 Cor. 6:20) "However I consider my life worth nothing to me; my only aim is to finish the race and complete the task the Lord Jesus has given me- the task of testifying to the Good News of God's grace." (Acts 20:24 NIV) Your responsibility in belonging to God is to testify of His goodness in your life. There is somebody somewhere that needs what you have already been given. Testify.

I AM PRECIOUS

*"Since **you were precious in My sight**, you have been honored, and I have loved you; therefore I will give men for you, and people for your life." Isaiah 43:4*

Of all God's creation- the moon, the stars, the galaxies, oceans and mountains, He calls *you* precious. Not cute and sweet precious, but precious as in *valuable*. Metals such as fine gold and platinum, and jewels such as rare diamonds, are referred to as precious. They're of greater value than other metals and jewels. God sees you that way. Think of your child. Your child is precious. No one else or no other thing could take their place. In reading the entirety of Isaiah 43, the thing that stands out most to me is that regardless of whatever you may face, God is with you, to protect you and to work all things together for your good. (Rom. 8:28) *All* things. You may not understand it when it happens, but God is saying to trust Him, no matter what it is, and He will be with you and work it out. I don't care how old you are, you're still God's precious baby. He wants you to be totally dependent on Him for everything, no matter how big or small it seems to you. There's another reason that you're precious to God. He invested in you. Jesus paid for you with His Blood. Now, you are an ambassador for Him. It's your job to know Him and make Him known, to be His hands and feet and heart in this world. Jeremiah 29:11 says that God has plans and a purpose for you. It's now *your* responsibility to fulfill those. God is looking for a return on His investment, and He gives you the Holy Spirit to help you. Good works won't get you into Heaven, but it will bring others with you when you do. When you come out of darkness into light, there's a natural response to want others to live in the light of God's glory, too. It's the natural outpouring of love for others. God fills you with so much love, it just naturally flows from you to others. That in itself is precious! It's precious to God and it's precious to the lives that are affected. God cares for you and loves you. You are precious above all else to Him.

I AM HONORED

"Since you were precious in My sight, **you have been honored,** *and I will give men for you, and people for your life." Isaiah 43:4*

Do you ever feel like you're passed by in opportunites where you should be recognized? Like you do all the work and other people get all the credit or benefits for it? Or how about shame? Do you feel shame over something you've done, or something that was done to you? First of all, God knows. He sees all and knows all. God sees how hard you're working, how hard you're trying, day in and day out, and He is the only one that you have to please. In time, God will honor you because God is all about justice. "And whatever you do, do it heartily, as to the Lord and not to men." (Col. 3:23) All reward comes from God, even if He uses someone to send it through. "Therefore, my beloved brethren, be steadfast, immovable, always abounding in the work of the Lord, knowing that your labor is not in vain in the Lord." Shame is the opposite of honor. Too often people carry shame from something someone else has done to them, things which were out of their control. You were never meant to carry that heavy load. "Come to Me, all you who labor and are heavy laden, and I will give you rest. Take My yoke upon you and learn from Me, for I am gentle and lowly in heart, and you will find rest for your souls. For My yoke is easy and My burden is light." (Mt. 11:28-

30) God is a man of His Word. If He says something, it is infallible. Psalm 91:15 says, "He shall call upon Me, and I will answer him; I will be with him in trouble; I will deliver him *and honor him.*" Let's break that down. Your role is to call upon the Lord. From there, God says He will answer you, He will be with you, He will deliver you, and He will *honor you.* If you've done your part, and God has delivered you from the trouble you were in, ask Him to honor you as well. Remind Him of His Word. When you pray, it's important to pray God's Word back to Him. He watches over His Word to perform it. (Jer. 1:12) And His Word never comes back to Him without doing what He says it will do. (Is. 55:11) Knowing who God says you are enables you to shake off shame and be clothed in honor, because that's who He created you to be.

I AM LOVED

*"Since you were precious in My sight, you have been honored, and **I** **have loved you**; therefore, I will give men for you, and people for your life." Isaiah 43:4*

The one thing I've always wanted was to be loved. I never felt loved, even by people that loved me, because I had no idea what love was and I didn't think I was lovable. I was searching for perfect love, and that's impossible to find outside of God's perfect love. The intense craving for love was actually an intense craving for God, because God is love. (1 Jn. 4:16) The emptiness that people try to fill with things can only be filled with God. It's a God shaped hole, which often becomes a God shaped vacuum. Trying to fill the hole with drugs or sex or money or food doesn't work. It may feel like it works, but it then becomes a vacuum which not only sucks in the things you're trying to fill it with, it also sucks in your very soul until you feel like there's no way out. Jesus is the Way, the Truth, and the Life. (Jn. 14:6) Everything Jesus did, He did in love. "But God demonstrates His own love toward us, in that while we were still sinners, Christ died for us." (Rom. 5:8) Even as Jesus hung on the Cross, He prayed for the people that nailed Him to it. (Lk. 23:34) God's love is unfathomable, unconditional, and immeasurable. It's based on who He is, not on you or anything you've ever done or not done. It never changes and it never ends. You just have to receive it. Allow his love to fill you up until you are overflowing with it. From this overflow, God will pour out His Spirit on the people around you. Loving others is part of God's plan, especially those who are at some disadvantage in life. "Freely you have received, freely give." (Mt. 10:8) God's love is so amazing. It gives life to the dead, healing to the sick, hope to the hopeless. It transforms hearts and minds and lives. You are a part of this life of love. You are at the very center of it, because God loves *you*.

I AM CARVED ON THE PALMS OF GOD'S HANDS

*"See, **I have inscribed you on the palms of My hands**; your walls are continually before Me." Isaiah 49:16*

Notice this verse doesn't say that God has inscribed, (engraved or carved), your name on the palms of His hands. It says that He has inscribed *you* on the palms of His hands. You and all that concerns you are in His hands. (Ps. 31:15) Think about having something carved into your hand. It would hurt. "And being found in appearance as a man, He humbled Himself and became obedient to the point of death, even the death of the Cross." (Php. 2:8) Jesus bore pain to the point of death because of His great love for you. Right alongside those scars where the nails were is a carving of you on His palm. That's love. Every time Jesus looks at His hands, He is reminded of you. When something tries to come against you, He can close His hand to make a fist, to keep you safe and protected, and He fights for you. Jesus says in John 10:29, "My Father, who has given them to Me, is greater than all, and no one is able to snatch them out of the Father's hand." God's hands are mighty. (1 Ptr. 5:6) God holds your hand like a small child and helps you. (Is. 41:13) In God's hands are power, safety, protection, deliverance, authority, favor, correction, and most of all, love. The inscription on God's hands can be likened to a mother having her children's names tattooed on her heart, except its God and His love is immeasurable and eternal. It's perfect in every way. The verse right before this one says, "Can a woman forget her nursing child, and not have compassion on the son of her womb? Surely they may forget, yet I will not forget you." (Is. 49:15) You are God's precious child. In light of eternity, you are still just a baby to Him. What you see as mistakes and failures, He sees as you growing and learning. He is there to help you grow. He's there to teach you and guide you. His hand is with you every baby step that you take. Sure, you'll fall down sometimes, and sure, it will hurt, but Daddy God will help you back up and tell you to try it again. When He holds His arms out for you to toddle into, take a look at His hands. It's *you*.

MY WALLS ARE CONTINUALLY BEFORE GOD

"See, I have inscribed you on the palms of My hands; **your walls are continually before Me***." Isaiah 49:16*

In ancient times, the walls of a city were its protection. If there was a breach in the walls, enemies could enter in and cause destruction. Your walls refer to your barrier of protection. God watches over you continually to protect you from things that you aren't even aware of. Remember, the enemy is not flesh and blood, but spirits who are sent by Satan. Your walls speak of your health, strength, prosperity, peace, and security. If there is an opening in any of those things, evil spirits can enter. Sin can create an opening, giving evil spirits a door by which to enter. God watches over you to protect you, but you have to be mindful to avoid sin, so that you aren't opening the door and inviting the devil in. Awe and respect for God causes Him to surround you and bring deliverance. God is for you. He will fight for you, and you shall hold your peace. (Ex. 14:14) That means stay out of His way and don't try to defend yourself. Trust God to be God. Think about the president. He has bodyguards, the Secret Service, to protect him. How foolish would it be for the president, with all that highly trained, professional security, to think he had to take part in protecting himself? Yet that's basically what people do when they don't trust and obey God. Within your walls, the atmosphere should be one of peace, and righteousness should flow like a river. God will protect that because that's His will for those who seek to have a relationship with Him, to follow His ways, and live according to His will. God Himself is your wall, your defense against the enemy. Psalm 91:1-2 comes to mind, "He who dwells in the secret place of the Most High shall abide under the shadow of the Almighty. I will say of the Lord, "He is my Refuge and my Fortress; my God, in Him I will trust."" In Job 1:10, Satan asks God, "Have You not made a *hedge around him, around his household, and around all that he has on every side?"* God had a wall of protection around Job because Job "feared God and shunned evil". (Job 1:1) Your walls are in the very presence of Almighty God, and you are safe there.

I AM THE BRIDE OF CHRIST

*"For **your Maker is your Husband**, the Lord of Hosts is His Name; and your Redeemer is the Holy One of Israel; He is called the God of the whole earth." Isaiah 54:5*

I was in a toxic, abusive relationship and saw no way out. I was about to be evicted and had nowhere to go. I cried out to God and asked Him to get rid of the man *for me*. And He did. I still was faced with eviction. I asked Jesus to be my Husband, to love me and take care of me in the same way any husband would. And He did, only better. I poured over the Word, and Jesus met me there. He taught me that in ancient Jewish culture, the groom's father approached the bride's father to ask for marriage. If the bride's father accepted, a price was then paid to the father and gifts were given to the bride. The groom would then go back to his father's house and build an addition onto his father's house for the newlyweds to live in. The time was not known when the groom would return for his bride. Jesus taught me through revelation that, as His bride, I was given the gift of the Holy Spirit. Then He led me to John 14:1-3, "Let not your heart be troubled; you believe in God, believe also in Me. In My Father's house are many mansions, if it were not so, I would have told you. I go to prepare a place for you. And if I go to prepare a place for you, I will come again and receive you to Myself; that where I am, there you may be also." I had always thought that was about going to Heaven, and maybe it is, but Christ taught me that it's about the marriage home! In the story of Esther, the king was looking for a new wife. He had all the beautiful virgins brought to the palace and they were to be given beauty preparations for one year. How does God define beauty? A gentle and quiet spirit. (1 Ptr. 3:4) Holiness. (Ps. 96:9) Virtue, strength, intelligence, compassion, charity, honor, fear of the Lord, substance. (Prov. 31) Those are the beauty treatments to apply while you wait for your Husband. You are to remain faithful, committed, and watchful of His return. Jesus is a real man, and He is God, and you are so blessed to be the bride that He has chosen to fall in love with.

GOD IS MY FATHER

*"But now, O Lord, **You are our Father**; we are the clay, and You are our potter; and all we are the work of Your hand." Isaiah 64:8*

Did you know that your relationship with your earthly father can have a lot to do with how you see God? If you had an overbearing father, you tend to see God as a big, mean bully waiting to hit you over the head with a Bible. If you had a father who violated you, you tend to see God as uncaring and manipulative. If your father wasn't there, you might think that God isn't real. Even if you had a great father, he wasn't perfect, but God is. As your Creator, He made you. He formed you in the womb and even knew you before He formed you. (Jer. 1:5) 2 Corinthians 6:18 says, "I will be a Father to you, and you shall be My sons and daughters, says the Lord Almighty." Speaking of Christ, John 1:12 says, "But as many as received Him, to them He gave the right to become children of God, to those who believe in His Name." If you have received Jesus as your Lord and Savior, you are not merely God's creation, you are His child. He wants a relationship with you. That's what sets apart the creation from the child. Nonbelievers don't have or want a relationship with God. A child *does* want a relationship with their father. "Behold what manner of love the Father has bestowed on us, that we should be called children of God! Therefore the world does not know us, because it did not know Him." (1 Jn. 3:1) A good father provides for his children. God provided the ultimate sacrifice for you as His child. "For God so loved the world, that He gave His only begotten Son, that whoever believes in Him should not perish but have everlasting life." (Jn. 3:16) Ephesians 1:3-5 says, "Blessed be the God and Father of our Lord Jesus Christ, who has blessed us with *every spiritual blessing* in the Heavenly places in Christ, just as *He chose us in Him* before the foundation of the world, that we should be holy and without blame before Him in love, having predestined us *to adoption, as sons* by Jesus Christ to Himself, according to the good pleasure of His will." And most of all, a good father loves his children. "The Lord has appeared of old to me, saying, "Yes, I have loved you with an everlasting love; therefore with lovingkindness I have drawn you."" (Jer. 31:3) God's love is eternal. It existed long before the foundation of the world, and it will exist forever in eternity. Nothing will ever change that, child.

I AM THE WORK OF GOD'S HAND

*"But now, O Lord, you are our Father; we are the clay, and You are our potter; and all **we are the work of Your hand.**" Isaiah 64:8*

On people's birthdays, I like to send this quote that I found online: "How cool is it that the same God who created mountains, oceans, and galaxies looked at you and thought the world needed one of you, too!" That's pretty amazing. And it's very humbling. When a potter is making something with clay, he can always reshape it into something else. All he has to do is slam it down on a hard surface and start remolding it. Well, that's kind of how God does it, too. I know I've been going along doing my own thing, and next thing you know, bam! My life gets turned upside down and when I think it can't get any crazier, bam! Bam! Bam! And that's just the beginning. I stick it out. I shuffle things around. I cry. I put on a brave face. But then, I break down. I cry out to God. I pour out my soul to Him, and even though I've done whatever it was in disobedience, in unfaithfulness, in hardness of heart, He hears me and He rescues me. He sets me back on my feet, and starts remolding me into who He created me to be. This is where submission to God's will comes in. In order for you to be the vessel God created you to be, you must be submissive to His will. God's will is His Word. They never contradict one another. You have to stay in the Word of God to know His will and His ways. You were chosen to be a vessel of honor. 2 Timothy 2:20-21 says, "But in a great house there are not only vessels of gold and silver, but also of wood and clay, some for honor and some for dishonor. Therefore *if anyone cleanses himself from the latter, he will be a vessel for honor, sanctified and useful for the Master, prepared for every good work.*"And Psalm 50:23 says, "And to him who orders his conduct aright, I will show the salvation of God." In other words, when you repent of your own ways and the ways of the world, and leave that way of life behind to follow after God and His ways, God will help you, He will honor you, and He will use you for making a difference in this world. He will use you for His Kingdom, here in this earth. Your life will flourish under the mighty hand of the Potter. If God has delivered you, He will honor you. (Ps. 91:15) That's His Word! This life is what God created you for. It isn't always easy, but it's worth every minute of it, eternally.

I AM HEALED

*"Heal me, O Lord, and **I shall be healed;** save me, and I shall be saved, for You are my praise."* Jeremiah 17:14

Doctors can give you medicine or therapy for healing, but when God heals you, *you are healed and made whole!* The word "whole" in Greek means "to save, keep safe and sound, to rescue from danger or destruction". Healing means to make well, but to be healed and whole means that even the effects of the illness are no longer present. It means that you are healed inside and out, both physically and spiritually. Not many people survive spinal meningitis, or brain infections, or strokes. I had all of them at once. And lived. The doctors said that it was a miracle. I agree. Only God has the power to do miracles. I've known several people who were healed of HIV. None of them were on medications. Without exception, all of them are born again Christians. I was first saved from a life of drug addiction, which for me is no life at all. It's literally the living dead.

255

I don't think back on it, romancing the drug. I don't ever want it again. I stay true to the reality of what it really was. And I can't say that I've always been able to do that. It's all God. I'm no longer tormented by memories of violence and violation that I experienced in childhood. God's healing is complete. Healing is your covenant right as a believer. Jesus paid for your healing when He was beaten and hung on the Cross. If you go to the doctor's office, your insurance pays for your visit. It doesn't necessarily mean you will be healed. Jesus paid for your *healing*, in full. In almost every case where Jesus healed a person, He tells them, "*Your faith* has made you well." It's what you believe. I believe that, like the little girl in Mark 5:35-43, there were those who said I was dead, but Jesus showed up with Peter, James, and John, and my parents, who have gone on to Heaven, and said, "The child is not dead, but sleeping." And I believe He then told me, "Little girl, I say to you, arise." I have no doubt in my mind. It isn't enough to claim your healing. Receive it, believe it, and speak it. Do not agree with the devil! "Death and life are in the power of the tongue and those who love it shall eat its fruit." (Prov. 18:21) Be careful what fruit you are eating.

I AM SAVED

*"Heal me, O Lord, and I shall be healed; save me, and **I shall be saved**, for You are my praise." Jeremiah 17:14*

The word "saved" means rescued, delivered. Salvation includes redemption from sin and its consequences, such as death and separation from God. Christ saved you when He conquered sin and death on the Cross. I want to make something very clear. Once you are saved, you cannot lose your salvation. It unnerves me when I hear Christians, especially mature Christians, say, "I don't want to go to hell." Well, if you are saved, you won't. I don't care what you do. You may not get to the same place in Heaven that you may have gone, but you will not go to hell. When I was a little girl, I got saved at Vacation Bible School at the church where my babysitter went. When I went home, my daddy was yelling and saying cuss words. I thought that every time he said a cuss word and I heard it, that I was sinning, so I tried to say what I could remember of the prayer I had said to get saved. Over and over, every time I heard those words. It happened so much that I couldn't keep up and I thought I wasn't saved anymore. Throughout my life, I got saved many times, I thought, because I thought I had lost my salvation. Salvation comes through Jesus Christ, and Him crucified. (1 Cor. 2:2) Period. It has nothing to do with what you've done. It's all about what Jesus did.

(Eph. 2:8-9) "Neither is there salvation in any other; for there is none other Name under Heaven given among men, whereby we must be saved." (Acts 4:12) Once you're saved, you're saved. That doesn't mean that you can get saved and keep on sinning. "God is light, and in Him there is no darkness at all. If we say that we have fellowship with Him, and walk in darkness, we lie and do not practice the Truth. But if we walk in the light as He is in the light, we have fellowship with one another, and the Blood of Jesus Christ His Son cleanses us from all sin." (1 Jn. 1:5-7) Acts 16:30-31 says, "And he brought them out and said, "Sirs, what must I do to be saved?" So they said, "Believe on the Lord Jesus Christ, and you will be saved, you and your household." Did you get that? When you believe in Jesus, and confess Him as Lord of your life, (Rom. 10:9-10) you *and your household will be saved!* That means your spouse, your children, anyone else within your home, all will be saved, because of your decision to live for Christ. You are called to be light in a very dark world. That world starts at home.

I AM CREATED FOR A PURPOSE

"For I know the thoughts that I think toward you, says the Lord, ***thoughts of peace and not of evil, to give you a future and a hope."***
Jeremiah 29:11

Your life is not accidental. You were created very intentionally, very carefully, and you are here for a reason. One of those reasons is to have a real relationship with God. Another reason is to bring others into relationship with God. Another reason, "For we are His workmanship, *created in Christ Jesus for good works*, which God prepared beforehand that we should walk in them." (Eph. 2:10) There are people who need compassion, love, need their physical needs met, such as food, clothing, shelter, someone to listen to them. Those are simple things that aren't so commonly shared and the people who need them need them desperately. Good works won't get you into Heaven, only Jesus can do that, but it will share the love of Jesus with others and help them to know Him. God created you for His pleasure and His glory, so your life should be a reflection of that. And it will. God doesn't get any glory out of you living in sickness and poverty and turmoil until He brings you out of it. Spend quality time with God. Submit to Him, to His ways, to His Word. Doing so will enable Him to fulfill His plans and purposes for your life, and you will experience life like you never dreamed imaginable. Right

259

now, at this point in my life, I would have never dared to dream that I would just now come alive, with so many hopes for a future. I am *living* my life, the life that God intended for me from the very beginning of time, before the earth was even formed. The way you live your life is an act of worship. It puts God's glory on display for all the world to see. He intends for goodness in your life so that others will be drawn to what they see in you. Jesus.

I HAVE A FUTURE AND A HOPE

*"For I know the thoughts that I think toward you, says the Lord, thoughts of peace and not of evil, **to give you a future and a hope.**" Jeremiah 29:11*

Two years ago, I was in a horrible relationship. I was homeless, but a friend was letting my boyfriend and I sleep in his living room. I was sick and no one thought I would make it much longer. And I didn't care. I was tired of "living". I wasn't really living, just waiting for it to end. I cried out to God. For the first time ever, I asked Him to fulfill *His plans* for my life, and not my own. Next thing you know, the boyfriend got arrested and I ended up in a ministry that helped homeless people. It wasn't a coincidence. God moves things around to get His work done. I didn't think I would stay at the ministry very long, but it's more than a shelter. There are Bible studies every day, there's serving, there's growth and healing. I found that I was in a God centered environment that allowed me to develop my maturity as a Christian. I was able to grow into the person God created me to be. I had to grow into that person in order to fulfill His plans for me. This book is not for me. It's for Him, for His plans and purposes. My greatest desire for this book is for your life to be completely transformed by the power of God, to fulfill *His plans and purposes* for *your life*, whatever that may be. I never saw myself as anything other than who I used to be. God saw who He made me to be. He had a future in mind for me long before I did. His plans for my future gave me hope, because He showed Himself faithful to me time and time again. That enabled me to trust Him for bigger things. That's where my hope comes from. Not in my own ability. I was overwhelmed at one point, in writing this book. My mind raced with thoughts of "How can I do this? It's going to take forever. What if…" I stopped writing for 2 months. I finally realized that it was the devil putting those thoughts in my mind. Doubt, discouragement, fear. No, I can't do it, but God can. His Word says that with Him, *all* things are possible. (Mt. 19:26) Not some things, not just the easy things, but ALL things. And surely He will help me to fulfill *His plans and purposes* for my future. Where God guides, He provides. And He will do the same for you.

I AM NEVER ALONE

*"**The Lord your God in your midst**, the Mighty One, will save; He will rejoice over you with gladness, He will quiet you with His love, He will rejoice over you with singing."*   *Zephaniah 3:17*

The presence of God is so beautiful. He is always with you. Sometimes He makes it very noticeable, but what about those times when you don't feel Him or hear from Him or when you literally feel like He isn't there? You have to remind yourself to be strong and courageous, that God will *never* leave you. (Deut. 31:6) And keep reminding yourself until you know it without a doubt. I hear people say, "I've got chill bumps" or something to that effect, to describe the presence of the Holy Spirit, and that happens too, but even when it doesn't, He is still with you. He does manifest His presence in amazing ways, though. After church one day, I was sitting outside on a bench with my back facing the parking lot. I was facing a window and could see people walking behind me. I saw several couples holding hands and I thought, "That would be so nice." I closed my eyes and then I had the feeling of someone leaning against my back. I looked up into the window and only saw my own reflection, but then my arms felt as if someone were caressing my forearms, stroking them with their hands. Those times happen, too, and there's no way to describe the inestimable beauty of those moments. God is not far, far away. He is near to all who call on Him. (Ps. 145:18) Right now, He is with you. Hold out your hand. You are touching God! Place your hand on yourself. You are touching God. His Spirit lives within you. (2 Cor. 13:5) Jesus *lives inside of you.* He is literally in your midst. The midst of you, your life, your family, everything that concerns you. He walks with you, talks with you, loves you, helps you. Call on Him, speak to Him, all throughout the day and night. The Bible says in Proverbs 18:24 that Jesus is "a friend that sticks closer than a brother." There is no more perfect companion than Jesus.

GOD REJOICES OVER ME WITH GLADNESS

"The Lord your God in your midst, the Mighty One, will save; ***He will rejoice over you with gladness***, *He will quiet you with His love, He will rejoice over you with singing." Zephaniah* 3:17

The King James Version of this Scripture says, "He will rejoice over thee with joy." The word rejoice literally means "dance, skip, leap, and spin around in joy". Can you imagine that? Can you imagine anyone being that in love with you, but *God Himself* being that in love with you? My whole life I craved love. I thought if there were somebody, somewhere, who would love me like I knew I could love them, my life would be perfect. I looked for that love in relationships, but I could never find it because I didn't know what love was, and I thought I didn't deserve love, anyway. I settled for what I thought was love, but any love outside of family was anything but love. It wasn't until I asked Jesus to be a Husband to me, and even then, until I accepted it fully myself, that I knew what real love was. And I'm still learning. Surely God's love for me isn't based on anything I've done. God's love is based entirely on who He is. He *is* love. (1 Jn. 4:8) The love God has for you is unfathomable, but get a good mental picture of God getting a tattoo of you on the palm of His hand, dancing and whirling around, sweeping you up in His arms, and singing love songs to you at the top of His lungs. He's got pictures of you in His wallet. He's got a book with your name in it. (Php. 4:3) There are pictures of you all over His walls. He's so in love with you! You're His precious child. (Deut. 26:18) For a love so amazing, it should be your highest goal to love God back to your absolute fullest. 2 Corinthians 5:9 says, "Therefore we make it our aim, whether present or absent, to be well pleasing to Him." Faith is pleasing to God. (Heb. 11:6) Fear of the Lord and hope in Him are pleasing to God. (Ps. 147:11) Obedience is more pleasing to God than sacrifice. (1 Sam. 15:22) Repentance, turning away from sin, pleases God. (Ps. 51:16-17) Calling on God, spending time in His presence, delights the Lord. (Ps. 65:4) God rejoices over you just as you are, and your response should simply be an overwhelming desire to love Him back. That's His heart's desire.

GOD QUIETS ME WITH HIS LOVE

*"The Lord your God in your midst, the Mighty One, will save; He will rejoice over you with gladness, **He will quiet you with His love**, and He will rejoice over you with singing." Zephaniah 3:17*

In my own life, the life I used to live, there was very little quiet. Because of the lifestyle related to being a drug addict, even in quiet moments, I was tormented in my thoughts. Whether I had drugs or not, I was panicked, uneasy, fearful. My mind screamed at me, *especially* when it was quiet. No matter how long I had been awake, the quiet around me gave way to the voices coming from my own thoughts. I couldn't stop them. They were like the sound of a mob of people in the midst of some kind of attack. And there was the voice of my accuser, as well. I would relive every horrible thing I had ever experienced, especially things that happened in my childhood. I would relive every last detail, over and over. I wondered why I was doing that, but I couldn't stop. And then, through it all, I could hear a voice, accusing me, telling me that it was my fault, that I liked it, that that's all I was good for. But it was just me. These were *my* thoughts. Or were they? In Mark 5:1-20, Jesus encountered a man who was possessed by many demons. His name was Legion, "for we are many". (Mk. 5:9) Jesus cast the demons out of the man, and in verse 15 it says that he was "sitting and clothed and in his right mind". Revelation 12:10 calls Satan the accuser of the brethren. In Job 19:2, Job asks, "How long will you torment my soul, and break me in pieces *with words*?" Now look over in Job chapter 1. Satan goes before God to accuse Job and get permission to test Job. Throughout the book of Job, he suffered the loss of everything and everyone, except his wife and a few well-meaning friends, but even they accused Job of bringing on all that happened to him because he must have sinned. His wife even told him to go ahead and curse God and die! Job didn't sin against God and in the end, God blessed him more in his latter years than in the beginning. God quieted him with His love. He has done that for me, too, even though, unlike Job, I did sin. God, in His love, was merciful to me. I have peace, even when things aren't looking so good. My mind is sound. I want this for you. It belongs to you already. You are loved unconditionally. Everything that God has for you is already yours. Pursue those things with all your heart. Be quieted by the love God has for you.

GOD REJOICES OVER ME WITH SINGING

*"The Lord your God in your midst, the Mighty One, will save; He will rejoice over you with gladness, He will quiet you with his love, **He will rejoice over you with singing.**" Zephaniah 3:17*

When babies cry or are fussy, the people who love them and take care of them often sing over them to quiet them, to give them peace, and comfort them. So God does for us. Sometimes, your biggest tears are never seen by others. They're either shed in isolation or, if you're like me, you choked back tears with a smile on your face. Not because you are strong, but because you, too, refused to let anyone see how much they were hurting you. Believe me, I know. You may have fooled others, but God knows. He's the one who sang over you in those moments. That's where your peace and your strength came from. It's how you made it this far. You don't have to hold back anymore. Let it out, all of it. God collects your tears in a bottle and writes them down. "You number my wanderings; put my tears into Your bottle; are they not in Your book?" (Ps. 56:8) Every detail of your life is important to God. When you hurt, He hurts. I know that God has sang over me a lot because I have cried many, many tears. I wonder what He sings? What His voice sounds like? Nothing is hidden from God. Your innermost feelings, the thoughts that are too raw to even think about, the things they said or the things they did to you, God knows every one of them. And He is a God of justice and righteousness. You may never know or see it, but God will repay them. "Beloved, do not avenge yourselves, but rather give place to wrath; for it is written, "Vengeance is Mine, I will repay," says the Lord." (Rom. 12:19) You were never meant to carry that load. It's too heavy for you. Lay it at the feet of Jesus, and leave it there. You can't walk into the future God has in store for you carrying those heavy burdens. They don't belong to you anymore. Listen for God's voice, relax, and be comforted. Rest in His presence. Just be still, and know that He is *God*, strong and powerful, rich in mercy. "But

You, O Lord, are a God full of compassion, and gracious, longsuffering and abundant in mercy and truth." (Ps. 86:15) You are that crying, fussy baby. And it's okay. God is singing love songs over you, to comfort and quiet you. Rest in his love, child.

I AM THE SALT OF THE EARTH

"You are the salt of the earth; but if the salt loses its flavor, how shall it be seasoned? It is then good for nothing but to be thrown out and trampled underfoot by men." Matthew 5:13

This verse is from Jesus' Sermon on the Mount. During Biblical times, salt was very valuable. In fact, it was used as currency. The Roman soldiers received part of their pay in salt. That's where the word "salary" comes from. The people Jesus was preaching to that day were common people- farmers, shepherds, fishermen. The religious leaders were wealthy. They were "above" the common people. They depended on the Law of Moses and traditions of men to maintain their status. It was impossible to follow. What Jesus was saying to the people in this verse was that there was a new law, grace, and that under the new law, even the common people could be included, because they were as priceless to the Father as anyone else. In fact, they were specifically called by God to display His glory. God doesn't call the qualified. He qualifies the called. "Brothers, think of what you were when you were called. Not many of you were wise by human standards; not many were influential; not many were of noble birth. But God chose the foolish things of the world to shame the wise; God chose the weak things of the world to shame the strong. He chose the lowly things of this world and the despised things – and the things that are not – to nullify the things that are, so that no one may boast before Him." (1 Cor. 1:26-29 NIV) God isn't impressed by your title or your car or where you live. God is moved by your heart. If your heart is all in it for Him and His agenda, that "wow's" Him. No matter where you are in your walk, even if you have only taken baby steps, you are valuable to God. How valuable? Romans 5:8, "But God demonstrates His own love toward us, in that while we were *still sinners*, Christ died for us." Charles Spurgeon said it this way, "Consider how precious a soul must be, when both God and the devil are after it." Think on that.

I AM THE LIGHT OF THE WORLD

*"**You are the light of the world**. A city that is set on a hill cannot be hidden." Matthew 5:14*

Jesus said, "I have come as a light into the world, that whoever believes in Me should not abide in darkness." (Jn, 12:46) When you give your life to Christ, He literally lives inside of you. (Gal. 2:20) By His Spirit, light shines in you, through you, and all around you. It may or may not be visible to the naked eye, but it is visible in the spirit realm, especially in darkness. If you were in a very dark room, so dark that you couldn't see at all, and a tiny light came on, what would you do? You would move toward the light, right? That's what the light of Christ does in you. It draws those living in darkness to you. The purpose for that is to show others what Christ has done for you, giving them hope. When I had been at the ministry for a few months, another woman and I went to deliver food to people in the neighborhood we had both come from. I saw several people that I knew, but there was one man that I used to use drugs with that we stopped and gave food to. He had known me how I used to be. I still looked the same. That hadn't changed. We talked a few minutes, and as I was walking away, he called me to come back to him. He said, "You really have changed, haven't you? It's real." I told him yes, and that I would pray for him until the day I saw him again. He said,

"I know you will." I still haven't seen him, and I still pray that God will draw him to Him. The point is, he saw the light. He saw that coming out of a life of bondage to drugs, to live a life of total peace, was possible. You are a minister of reconciliation. (2 Cor. 5:18) That means your light, what God has done in your life, is to serve as a continuation of Jesus' ministry while He was here- to bring others to Christ. "Let your light so shine before men, that they may see your good works and glorify your Father in Heaven." (Mt. 5:16) Your life can preach a better sermon than your lips.

I LOVE MY ENEMIES

*"But I say to you, **love your enemies**, bless those who curse you, do good to those who hate you, and pray for those who spitefully use you and persecute you." Matthew 5:44*

When you love your enemies, you're showing them Christ's love for them. When you know who you are in Christ, it will enable you to see who others really are, even if they're "not there yet". Romans 12:17-18 says, "Repay no one evil for evil. Have regard for good things in the sight of all men. If it is possible, as much as it depends on you, live peaceably with all men." It can be hard to do, especially since the world around you isn't of the same mind. The way of the world says to fight, to defend, to get revenge, and to hurt people that hurt you. God is on your side, though. He says plainly in this verse how to love your enemies. Bless them, which means speak good things over them. Do good to them. Nothing will confound an enemy like doing something kind for them or giving them a small gift. Holding your peace and praying for them instead will make the biggest difference. When you turn that person over to God in prayer, it becomes His responsibility. I used to have a person where I was serving at church that constantly stayed on me about every little nit-picky thing he could find. I truly was doing my best, but it was never good enough, never right. It was discouraging. I talked bad about him, talked bad to him. One night after I had been especially disrespectful to him, the Holy Spirit convicted me. He was in authority over me. Whether he was right or wrong, I had no right to be disrespectful to him. The next day I apologized and in those two days, I prayed over the situation quite a bit. For the next couple of weeks, every time I thought about the man, or every time my eyes saw him, I prayed for him. I also prayed for him every morning and every night. It made a difference. Judas Iscariot betrayed Jesus, unto Jesus' death. Jesus knew all along that he would, yet He loved Judas.

Jesus loved the ones who sent Him to the Cross, the ones who pounded the nails into His hands, the ones who beat Him and spit on Him and made fun of Him. Love is who Jesus is. He can't *not love*. Jesus died just as much for the sins of those who killed Him as He did for anyone else, and the love it took to do that conquered sin and death forever. That same love was resurrected with Jesus, so that you, too, could truly love your enemies and be a blessing in the earth, your Father's child.

I BLESS THOSE WHO CURSE ME

*"But I say to you, love your enemies, **bless those who curse you**, do good those who hate you, and pray for those who spitefully use you and persecute you." Matthew 5:44*

To bless someone means to speak good over them, which means *not* to turn right around and say something nasty about them. If someone speaks bad to you or over you, rebuke those words in the Name of Jesus, and speak a blessing over that person. It could be as simple as "God bless them" or you can find a Scripture, such as Numbers 6:24-26, to speak over them. You could even just say, "I forgive that person. I love them, and God, I ask you to bless them." Anything positive that you can think of to say about them is a blessing. Do not speak one negative word about them. Even if you can't think of any true statement concerning that person, speak good anyway. Romans 4:17 says, "God , who gives life to the dead and calls those things which do not exist as though they did." When you speak the Word of God over a person or situation, you are prophesying, declaring the Truth as God spoke it, and bringing life. You are literally declaring the life of God's Word to that person or circumstance. You are applying it, not like makeup, which only covers the surface, but like medicine, which is healing. Another way to bless someone is to do something kind for them. Ask God how you can be a blessing for that person, and don't be surprised if His answer is something you never would have expected. There's no telling what the other person may be going through that no one else knows about. A lot of times that's the whole reason people are agitated and stressed out, because they're dealing with stuff that nobody knows about. We all are to some extent, but there are some people that are carrying much heavier loads than others. Sharing the love of Jesus is what we're here to do. Mean people suck, but mean Christians are even worse. Speak this over yourself often, "I am patient, I am kind. I do not envy, I do not boast, I am not proud. I am not rude, I am not self-seeking, I am not easily angered, I keep no record of wrongs, I do not delight in evil, I rejoice in the Truth. I always protect, always trust, always hope, always persevere." That's from 1 Corinthians 13:4-7, which is about love. Love never fails. (1 Cor. 13:8)

I DO GOOD TO THOSE WHO HATE ME

*"But I say to you, love your enemies, bless those who curse you, **do good to those who hate you**, and pray for those who spitefully use you and persecute you." Matthew 5:44*

Hate is a strong word. It's a strong spirit. When Jesus was arrested, those people hated him. They mocked Him. They beat Him. They spit on Him. And they killed Him. He didn't open His mouth, except to pray for them. He responded in love. That's what you're called to do, too, especially if you're hated for your faith. "Blessed are those who are persecuted for righteousness' sake, for theirs is the Kingdom of Heaven. Blessed are you when they revile and persecute you, and say all kinds of evil against you falsely for My sake. Rejoice and be exceedingly glad, for great is your reward in Heaven, for so they persecuted the prophets who were before you." (Mt. 5:10-12) When someone seems determined to make your life miserable, that's persecution. Your response should be one of love and prayer. If it's a situation where you are being abused, you need to leave immediately, whatever you think it may cost you. God is with you and He will never leave you or forsake you. He is on your side. But if it isn't an abusive situation, but one that really does make you think that person hates you, do everything you can to respond with love and blessings. Turning the other cheek isn't weakness, by any means. It takes strength courage, and humility to walk away. Being Christlike is far from easy, but pleasing God is worth everything you go through along the way. Jesus could have called on thousands of hosts of angels, but He was more concerned about fulfilling God's will to atone for the sins of all the world. Jesus endured. He suffered. There are going to be times where you have to fight your flesh and just keep going. Keep pushing through. Keep praying and believing and trusting God. It isn't the person, but a spirit working through that person, that hates you. "If the world hates you, you know that it hated Me before it hated you. If you were of the world, the world would love its own. Yet, because you are not of the world, but I chose you out of the world, therefore the world hates you." Evil spirits recognize the Spirit of Christ, even when people don't. So bless the *person* and rebuke the spirit.

I PRAY FOR THOSE WHO SPITEFULLY USE ME AND PERSECUTE ME

*"But I say to you, love your enemies, bless those who curse you, do good to those who hate you, and **pray for those who spitefully use you and persecute you**." Matthew 5:44*

To pray for someone who has intentionally hurt you is in direct opposition to the natural response of seeking revenge. The Kingdom of God operates in ways that don't make logical sense to the human mind. ""For My thoughts are not your thoughts, nor are your ways My ways", says the Lord." The natural response is your flesh. The Kingdom of God is spiritual. When you crucify your flesh and respond in the Spirit, you are giving that situation to God. Exodus 14:14 says, "The Lord will fight for you, and you shall hold your peace." That means that you don't even open your mouth, except to pray. "I say then: walk in the Spirit, and you shall not fulfill the lust of the flesh." (Gal. 5:16) In such a situation, ask God to open that person's eyes to see the hurt that they have caused you, and to lead them to turn from those ways. Forgive that person. Have mercy on them, just like God had mercy on you. Yes, even when you didn't deserve it, either. God may even reveal something about your own actions that provoked that person. Pray that no one else is harmed by that person, and that God send someone to share the love of Jesus with them. That person may even be you. When you respond in love, it speaks louder than words. The Reverend Dr. Martin Luther King maintained a non-violent response to violent hatred. He is quoted, "Returning hate for hate multiplies hate, adding deeper darkness to a night already devoid of stars. Darkness cannot drive out darkness; only light can do that. Hate cannot drive out hate; only love can do that." Jesus Christ is light and love. His non-violent response to violent hatred is our example. I'm not saying it's easy. It isn't. Christ endured hatred, sin, sickness, suffering, and death, not so that you wouldn't have to, but so that you would know how to. John 13:35 says, "By this all will know that you are My disciples, if you have love for one another."

I LOVE THE LORD MY GOD WITH ALL MY HEART, WITH ALL MY SOUL, WITH ALL MY MIND, AND WITH ALL MY STRENGTH

"And you shall love the Lord your God with all your heart, with all your soul, with all your mind, and with all your strength. This is the first commandment." Mark 12:30

The first Bible study I ever gave was on this verse. I studied it for weeks. At the ministry I'm in, we say this as a part of our morning prayer. As I studied, I started asking myself, "Do we really know what this means, or are we just saying it because it's what we're supposed to say? I want to love the Lord to the fullest, so I looked into what this verse *really* means. The meaning of the word "heart" here, in the Greek, means your mind, or your thoughts and feelings. It's your responsibility to guard your mind against ungodly or worldly thoughts or feelings. You do this by declaring the Truth of the Word of God. When wrong or negative thoughts or feelings happen, you say, "I cast down every argument and high thing that exalts itself against the knowledge of God. I bring every thought captive to the obedience of Jesus Christ, in Jesus' Name." The meaning of the Greek word for "soul" is spirit. You must continually strive to walk in the Spirit. It isn't a one time deal. It takes focus and determination. Walking in the Spirit means to deny the flesh. Prayer and fasting helps you rely on the Spirit, rather than the flesh. Listen closely for the prompting of the Holy Spirit. The Greek word for mind means "understanding", or what you think about. Meditate on the Word of God. Choose a Scripture and roll it around in your mind. Think on it. Job 28:28 also says that understanding is to turn from evil. Repenting, or turning away from sin, shows your commitment to God, and therefore your love for Him. The Greek word for "strength" is power, ability, might. This is your physical body. "Or do you not know that your body is the temple of the Holy Spirit who is in you, whom you have from God, and you are not your own?" (1 Cor. 6:19) The pursuit of health and holiness glorify God. The summary of all this is to love God with your total being. Everything concerning you is to love the Lord God. "Therefore, whether you eat or drink, or whatever you do, do all to the glory of God." (1 Cor. 10:31) God is the air that you breathe, the food that you eat, your everything at all times in every way.

I LOVE MY NEIGHBOR AS MYSELF

"And the second, like it, is this: **'You shall love your neighbor as yourself.'** *There is no other commandment greater than these."*
Mark 12:31

I've never been much of a people person. In the past, my interpretation of this verse was, "Don't bother me and I won't bother you." God changed that. First of all, He told me one day that an isolated Christian is a useless Christian. I've learned, too, that an isolated Christian doesn't grow and mature very much. Being a loner made my whole world revolve around *me*. It doesn't make sense to the natural mind, but putting others before yourself, out of love, really does do what people seek in putting themselves first. And it's God's will. "Do nothing out of selfish ambition or conceit, but in humility consider others better than yourself. Each of you should look not only to your own interests, but also to the interests of others." (Php. 2:3-4) How does self indulgence *really* feel? Honestly? When I came to live at the ministry, I was surrounded by women. There was nowhere to have privacy, nowhere to have a moment of total silence. I had no choice but to deal with it. The ministry serves the homeless on the streets of Atlanta, and I had to learn to get along with other people in the ministry in order to be a part of serving the people that depended on the ministry for food, hygiene products, clothing, and blankets. Their need for those things was greater than my need for peace and quiet. I've been on those same streets and I know how it feels to be hungry, soaking wet, dirty, cold. I know what it feels like to think that no one cares. I know what it feels like to be out there and wonder if God could see me, and if He did, if He would send someone to help me. I rarely go out to serve the homeless myself, so I never even see the people I serve, but those are my "neighbors". Jesus said, "I tell you the truth, whatever you did for one of the least of these brothers of Mine, you did for Me." (Mt. 25:40 NIV) The homeless, the sick, those in prison, those are your neighbors, too. They need compassion, they need their physical, emotional, and spiritual needs met, probably more so than you can ever imagine. In meeting their needs, God brings you into a place of true love and fulfillment, both for others and yourself.

I GIVE AND IT IS GIVEN TO ME

"Give, and it will be given to you; good measure, pressed down, shaken together, and running over will be put into your bosom. For with the same measure that you use, it will be measured back to you." Luke 6:38

Universal laws are laws that govern the universe. They are unchangeable. Such laws include the laws of gravity, physics, polarity, cause and effect. There are universal spiritual laws as well. The law of sowing and reaping, or seed time and harvest time, is one of the universal spiritual laws. Luke 6:38 is based on the law of sowing and reaping. Have you ever heard the phrase, "You reap what you sow"? If you plant seeds of kindness, you can expect kindness in return. You don't get apples from watermelon seeds. Seeds take time to grow. What you plant today, you will harvest at a future time. It isn't usually immediate. Matthew 7:12 (MSG) says, "Here is a simple, rule-of-thumb guide for behavior: Ask yourself what you want people to do for you, then grab the initiative and do it for them. Add up God's Law and Prophets and this is what you get." Luke 6:38 is talking about judgment and forgiveness. (Lk. 6:37) When you plant seeds of forgiveness, you get forgiveness in return. When you plant seeds of judgment, you are judged in return. Many seeds produce fruit that carry more than one seed inside them. When you plant one act of charity, that seed, when full grown, will produce much more fruit. "But the fruit of the Spirit is love, joy, peace, longsuffering, kindness, goodness, faithful, gentleness, self-control. *Against* such there is *no law*." (Gal. 5:22-23) The sowing and reaping of the fruit of the Spirit is an immutable, universal law which no other law can change or stand against. Galatians 6:7-9 (NIV) says, "Do not be deceived: God cannot be mocked. A man reaps what he sows. The one who sows to please his sinful nature, from that nature will reap destruction; the one who sows to please the Spirit, from the Spirit will reap eternal life. Let us not become weary in doing good, for at the proper time we will reap a harvest if we do not give up." Keep doing good. Keep believing. Keep planting seeds. Your harvest is coming.

I HAVE AUTHORITY OVER ALL THE POWER OF THE ENEMY

*"Behold, **I give you the authority** to trample on serpents and scorpions, and **over all the power of the enemy**, and nothing shall by any means hurt you." Luke 10:19*

If I stand in the middle of the street and stop traffic, I'm going to have a lot of people ignore me, blow their horns at me, and yell at me. If a police officer stands in the street stopping traffic, traffic stops, because the police officer has been given authority to write tickets or arrest anyone that doesn't stop. Jesus gives you power over the devil and every demon that tries to come against you. It's your responsibility to use that power. Notice this verse says that *you* have authority over *all* the power of the enemy. Satan will come against you every conceivable way he can, but your response determines the outcome. Jesus gave you *His* authority, His Blood, His Name, and His Word to fight every scheme of the devil. Plead the Blood of Jesus over yourself, your family, and everything that concerns you every day. Plead the Blood of Jesus *against* every form of evil that tries to come against you. Don't give in and don't give up. Philippians 2:10 says, "That at the Name of Jesus every knee should bow, of those in Heaven, and of those on earth." You can usually tell you're under spiritual attack if it seems like things are coming at you quickly, all at once. The devil tries to overwhelm you by bombarding you. Another way the devil tries to attack is by rushing you. God doesn't rush you. The devil also tries to make you doubt what you believe. Always check your thoughts against the Word of God. God will never go against His Word. You are not powerless. You are strong in the Lord and in the power of *His might*. ((Eph. 6:10) Your Bible is your Sword. Speak the Word of God over yourself and over every situation, using the Word as a weapon against the enemy. Put on the whole armor of God daily. (Eph. 6:10-20) Praise God because worship is a powerful weapon. Walk in the Spirit and do not fulfill the lusts of the flesh. (Gal. 5:16) Walk in love. (Eph. 5:2) Walk in light. "For you were once in darkness, but now you are light in the Lord. Walk as children of light (for the fruit of the Spirit is in all goodness, righteousness, and truth), finding out what is acceptable to the Lord. And have no fellowship with the unfruitful works of darkness, but rather expose them." (Eph. 5:8-11) Spiritual warfare is real. You are more than equipped to live the life God has prepared for you. You are a mighty warrior in the army of the Lord.

NOTHING SHALL BY ANY MEANS HURT ME

*"Behold, I give you the authority to trample on serpents and scorpions, and over all the power of the enemy, and **nothing shall by any means hurt you.**" Luke 10:19*

The Bible tells us over and over again, "Fear not, for I (God) am with you." Fear will come, but it doesn't have to overtake you. I was paralyzed by fear most of my life. I didn't realize that worry only compounded fear. In fact, most of the things I feared never even happened. Now, when I'm facing scary situations, I remember Jesus' promise in this verse. If I live through it, good. And if I die, I will be in Heaven with Jesus and all my family that's already gone there. That gave me the courage to take a new approach to fear. Look it in the eye and tackle it head on, like a deadly force of destruction. And you know what? It works. "For the Word of God is living and powerful, and sharper than *any* two edged sword, piercing even to the division of soul and *spirit*, and of joints and marrow, and is a discerner of thoughts and intents of the heart. And there is *no creature hidden from His sight*, but *all* things are naked and open to the eyes of *Him to whom we must give account*." (Heb. 4:12-13) In other words, even the devil and his demons have to answer to the Word of God. Jesus says in John 16:33 that you *will* experience tribulation, or trials, but He commands us to "be of good cheer, I have overcome the world." In Matthew 10:16, Jesus says, "Behold, I send you out as sheep in the midst of wolves. Therefore be wise as serpents and harmless as doves." Have no fear, but use wisdom. Don't allow the enemy to intimidate you. Whatever has held you back from God's best for you, go after it with bulldog tenacity. God is with you. His Spirit is inside you. You have the Blood of Jesus covering you and the Word of God as your weapon. You have been given authority in Jesus' Name to give orders, make decisions, and enforce obedience according to God's will and His Word. Jesus' authority gives you power to do those things. He has already won the battle, but He graciously allows time to give everyone the opportunity to come to repentance, so that none should perish. (2 Ptr. 3:9)

I AM A CHILD OF GOD

"But as many as received Him, to them He gave the right to become ***children of God,*** *to those who believe in His Name;" John 1:12*

My favorite version of this verse is from the Message Bible. "But whoever did want Him, who believed He was who He claimed and would do what He said, He made to be their true selves, their child-of-God selves." Everyone who calls on the Name of the Lord will be saved. (Rom. 10:13) Salvation is irrevocable. It can't be taken away from you, no matter what you do, but there are different levels of living the God-life that come with salvation. A person who simply says the prayer of salvation and goes on as usual will have a much different experience than a person who has a hunger for the things of God and carrying out His will on earth. We are all God's creation. We are not all His children. Becoming God's child is the result of *receiving Jesus and believing in His Name.* The King James Bible says that God gives us "power" to become His children. In the Greek, that power is defined as "privilege, force, capacity, competency, freedom, delegated influence, authority, strength". When you become God's child, you don't just get a place in Heaven. You get all the promises of God, all the spiritual power, all of the blessings. It's your responsibility as a child of God to use those gifts for the benefit of others, in accordance with God's plans and purposes. Love, compassion, kindness, righteousness, and peace, are all God's will. Bringing as many others out of darkness into the light of Christ is most certainly God's will. You are called to live a Christ like life. The more you spend time with your new family, the more you will take on their characteristics. There were lots of people back in Jesus' day that didn't believe Him, didn't want Him around, didn't believe He could do the things He did. There still are. But not you. Praise the Lord that you are His beloved child, that you believe and receive Jesus by faith, and that you are finally coming into the life that God planned for you from the beginning. Not just when you get to Heaven, but here and now. Welcome home, child.

I AM BORN AGAIN

*"...**who were born**, not of blood, nor of the will of the flesh, nor of the will of man, but **of God**." John 1:13*

To be born of God is to be born again. In John chapter 3, Jesus is explaining rebirth to Nicodemus. In verses 5-7, Jesus tells him, "Most assuredly, I say to you, unless one is born of water and the Spirit, he cannot enter the Kingdom of God. That which is born of the flesh is flesh, and that which is born of the Spirit is spirit. Do not marvel that I say to you, 'You must be born again'." Being born of water is a reference to being born in the flesh. You are a spirit living in a body of flesh and blood. With that birth comes water. Water also is a symbolic reference to the Word of God and baptism. Being born of the Spirit is the rebirth. You no longer live *by* the flesh, but *in* the flesh only. The Holy Spirit lives inside you when you believe in the Name of Jesus and receive Him as the Son of God. I was saved when I was a child, at Vacation Bible School. I was born again many years later, while I was in jail, waiting to go prison. I *experienced* God. I didn't just hear about Him or read about Him. I literally experienced Him. I didn't know what had happened. I went to a woman that I saw reading her Bible a lot and tried to explain it. She told me that I had a revelation. I said, "No. I was reading Matthew." I didn't even know what a revelation was. God *revealed Himself* to me through

His Spirit and His Word. Because I received this personally, I didn't have to *try* to believe. I *knew*! It was undeniable. But I was still very much caught up in my flesh. The Spirit transforms the flesh, and it takes time. The lady I had asked about what happened got me a Bible and I started reading it. For the first time ever, I understood it. I didn't try to change my flesh, but the Spirit within me did that. I didn't even know it was something that I needed to do. Romans 12:1-2 says, "I beseech you therefore, brethren, by the mercies of God, to present your bodies as a living sacrifice, holy, acceptable to God, which is your reasonable service. And do not be conformed to this world, but be transformed by the renewing of your mind, that you may prove what is that good and acceptable and perfect will of God." Every bit of what that meant for me came by the reading of the Word. The Word of God and the Spirit of God renewed my mind *and* my flesh. Ask God to fill you with His Spirit. "Whoever believes that Jesus is the Christ is born of God." (1 Jn. 5:1)

I HEAR CHRIST'S WORD AND BELIEVE IN GOD

*"Most assuredly, I say to you, **he who hears My Word and believes in Him who sent Me** has everlasting life, and shall not come into judgment, but has passed from death into life." John 5:24*

Jesus Christ *is* the Living Word of God. (Jn. 1:1) Every page, from Genesis 1:1 to Revelation 22:21, is the Word of Christ. Jesus

Himself is the Author and Finisher of your faith. (Heb. 12:2) Faith is the same thing as believing. "So then faith comes by hearing, and hearing by *the Word of God.*" (Rom. 10:17) Your faith to believe in God comes from hearing the Word of God. The more time you spend reading and studying your Bible, the more you will believe the Word and put your trust in God. Your beliefs follow what your mind focuses on. When you read the Bible, whose voice do you hear? Your own. You believe your own voice above every other voice, which is why the devil tries to speak lies into your mind *using your voice.* When you take the Word from head knowledge to heart knowledge, it builds your belief system, which then manifests into your body and your life, and ultimately, overflows to the people around you. You are assured of eternal life. You are a new creation. "Therefore, if anyone is in Christ, he is a new creation; old things have passed away; behold, all things have become new." (2 Cor. 5:17) What does passed away mean? Dead. You are a new creation because of the Spirit which gives you life. You literally, spiritually, pass from death into life. I can tell you from my own experience it feels like I've passed from the walking dead to real life in the physical as well. I've had more worthwhile achievements in the last 2 years than I've had in my entire life, all put together. I give God the glory for every bit of it. And when I say "achievements", I don't mean it in the way I used to think of accomplishments. Not accolades or recognition, but fulfillment, purpose, the ability to do things I always wanted to do but never could. I've been writing since I was a child, but I've never finished anything. This devotional seemed to write itself during the initial writing. And this was *after* being in a coma, having a stroke, and being delivered from real, physical death. And serving within the ministry full time. God revealed to me why it flowed so easily. Everything that I had ever written was written for my own sake. This devotional was being written for the glory of God and His intended purposes. Amen! The Bible is where you find God as well as your own true self, the self that God created you for. Live that life to its absolute fullest.

I HAVE EVERLASTING LIFE

*"Most assuredly, I say to you, he who hears My Word and believes in Him who sent Me **has everlasting life** and shall not come into judgment, but has passed from death into life." John 5:24*

In John 6:56, Jesus tells His disciples, "He who eats my flesh and drinks My Blood abides in Me, and I in him." He was speaking metaphorically, but many of Jesus' own disciples were offended by their understanding of what He said and left Him. He asked the ones remaining if they wanted to leave, too. Peter responded by saying, in verse 68, "Lord, to whom shall we go? You have the Words of eternal life." There is only one way to the Father, only way to eternal life, and that's through the Son of God, Jesus Christ. "I am the Way, the Truth, and the Life. *No one comes to the Father except through Me.*" (Jn. 14:6) If you have received Jesus into your life, you have everlasting life. I used to have no fear of death because all I was doing was waiting to die, anyway. Life was hard and every day was a struggle. The only reason I didn't end it was because I knew I had caused enough pain to my family, and even though I saw no other way to end that pain other than killing myself so they wouldn't be put through any more, I knew that they wouldn't understand that. So I kept going. I still have no fear of death, but it's because now I know that Jesus conquered death and I'm going to live *forever.*

Living my life isn't a struggle anymore because I've surrendered all that I am, all that I do, all that I have, to Jesus, to do whatever He wants to with it. My everlasting life doesn't start when I die in the flesh, it starts when I receive Jesus and die in *the spirit*, allowing His Spirit to take over. I had desperately wanted to get off drugs, get out of the lifestyle I was in, but nothing, absolutely nothing, that I tried to do worked. When I surrendered to Jesus, He did it for me. He took on the job of cleaning me up, over time, one thing after another. God doesn't just drop all His blessings on you at once because He wants you to *know* that it was *Him* who did it and not you yourself. (Deut. 6:10-12) He also wants you to mature, and to do that, you just have to go through some things. He is preparing you for eternal life, everlasting life in His presence. "God will wipe away every tear from their eyes; there shall be no more death, nor sorrow, nor crying. There shall be no more pain, for the former things have passed away." (Rev. 21:4) All those things have to be finished here. Everlasting life is Paradise. Perfection. Earth is simply the place of refining.

I SHALL NOT COME INTO JUDGEMENT

*"Most assuredly, I say to you, he who hears My Word and believes in Him who sent Me has everlasting life and **shall not come into judgment**, but has passed from death into life."*   John 5:24

I can't find anywhere in the Bible that says that *believers* will have to account for their lives on judgment day. I know, this is a popular belief, that everyone has to stand before God on judgment day, but the Bible says that we (believers) are not under condemnation (Rom. 8:1) and we have been justified, or cleared, of all wrongdoing, because of our *faith*. (Rom. 5:1) Just like eternal life begins when you receive Jesus as your Lord and Savior, your justification begins then, too. That doesn't mean that you can do whatever you want to. It also doesn't mean that you won't mess up. It means that from the point of salvation, the Holy Spirit is working inside you to help you do the things that you should do and not do the things that you shouldn't. You still have to do your part, though. The Holy Spirit even helps you to do that. He gives you the desire to want to change according to God's will. One way to do that is to really get into the Bible. God will speak to you there, not only through the words on the pages, but also by His Spirit, "between the lines". That's revelation, when God reveals the secret things to you. When God forgives your sins, He also forgets them. "For I will be merciful to their unrighteousness, and their sins and their lawless deeds I will remember no more." (Heb. 8:12) If that is true, and it is, then why would a believer have to account for it later? I recently had all of my jail and prison records expunged. There were almost 50 charges that were following me around, even though I haven't been in any trouble whatsoever in 3 years. As it stands, my entire record is now cleared. I have been *justified*. My past can't ever be held against me. Do you honestly think that I would jeopardize that freedom by purposefully doing anything illegal? I have been given new life, both legally and spiritually. (Rom. 6:4) And *all* of it is a gift from God. (Jms. 1:17) You are a believer and you will not come under eternal judgment, because of what Jesus has *already* done for you. God's plan is for you to spend eternity with Him, and that plan started the moment you received Him unto salvation.

I HAVE PASSED FROM DEATH TO LIFE

"Most assuredly, I say to you, he who hears My Word and believes in Him who sent Me has everlasting life, and shall not come into judgment, but has passed from death into life." John 5:24

I've said it before and I'm going to say it again. My "life" up until I was born again was just a series of going through the motions as best as I could. I was the walking dead. After I was born again, I was able to take my first breaths of fresh air. It wasn't until I came out of a coma that I truly began to *live*, and even then I had to rehabilitate first. I had to learn to walk again, and chew and swallow and use my hands. As part of the trauma, I experienced PTSD. I had very vivid memories of being in a spiritual realm, with both demons and angels. I had knowledge of things that I had no way of knowing, such as someone with an infection in their legs. This was confirmed to me after I was released from the hospital, but I told some people about it when they visited me in the hospital. They were aware of the infection, but didn't let me know about it until I came home. No one expected me to live, but God performed a miracle in me. He gave me new life. As I approach my 56th birthday, I feel like this is just the beginning. Even as a child, I did not run. I would look at the other kids running around screaming their heads off, going nowhere, and think, "What are they doing?" A few months after I was released from the hospital, I did a 5K race. I didn't run all of it, but I DID A 5K! That was a *huge* deal for me. When I hit the halfway mark and turned to go back to the starting point, Galatians 2:20 started playing in my mind, over and over. "I have been crucified with Christ; it is no longer I who live, but Christ lives in me; and the life which I now live in the flesh I live by faith in the Son of God, who loved me and gave Himself for me." The thing is, *I didn't know that Scripture by heart.* But the Holy Spirit inside me knows it and repeated it to me the entire time. By the time I hit the finish line, I had an understanding that whether my body had physically died or not, *something did,* and I was not "me" anymore. It was like one of those old black and white Twilight Zone shows where a brain is put in another person's body and the person becomes whoever the brain used to belong to. The difference was that the "brain" was the Spirit of Jesus Christ, and I owed Him my very life. I was literally to be His hands, feet, mouth, heart, arms, legs, and eyes. My physical body was His to use for *His* plans and purposes. It's the same with you, too. Jesus gives you new life, real life, *His life,* to bring His Kingdom to this world, *through you.*

I ABIDE IN JESUS' WORD

*"Then Jesus said to those Jews who believed Him, "If you **abide in My Word**, you are My disciples, indeed.""* *John 8:31*

To abide means "to remain in, to dwell in, to *endure in*". The Bible isn't just a book. It's a living Spirit, (Jn. 6:63) the Spirit of Jesus Christ. (Jn. 1:1) To abide in Jesus' Word is to *continue in Christ's presence*. That means that you don't sporadically read the Bible, here and there. You don't just look for God's presence when you go to church. The Spirit of God is with you continually. When you *abide* in God's Spirit, you are aware of His continual presence (whether you *feel it* or not) and you respond to it, you acknowledge it, you depend on it. You also seek it out, *especially* when you don't feel it. In the past, I've had "dry seasons" where I didn't feel God's presence, didn't hear His voice, but I learned to push through those periods by increasing my Bible reading and reminding myself that just because I didn't sense God during that time, it didn't mean He wasn't there. His Word says He will *never* leave me and that I am never alone. Just because I can't see or feel Him doesn't change the Truth. In those times when it feels like God isn't there, it's important to will myself to believe otherwise. It's also a red flag that I need to spend more time in the Word. Jeremiah 29:13 promises, "And you will seek Me and find Me, when you search for Me with all your heart." I endure, trusting the Lord to fulfill His promise. I keep pushing, no matter what it looks like, what it feels like, or how hard it is. There's a saying, "When you are going through something hard and wonder where God is, remember the teacher is always quiet during a test." Sometimes, that's what it's all about. Whether you pass your test or not depends on you. You may as well give it your best shot, because if you fail, you're just going to have to take it again. Remember the Israelites in the wilderness? They circled that mountain 40 years. It should have only taken them 11 days. God is patient. He wants you to get it right. And He wants you to trust Him. He wants you to spend eternity with Him. Eternity starts now.

I AM A DISCIPLE OF JESUS CHRIST

*"Then Jesus said to those Jews who believed Him, "If you abide in My Word, **you are My disciples, indeed**." John 8:31*

There were many followers of Jesus, and many disciples. There still are. The difference is that a follower of Jesus may just warm a pew in church occasionally, or even often, and truly believe that that makes them in right standing with God. But what happens when church is over? Maybe they live a bright, shiny life that looks good, looks upright, but that isn't enough. The disciples were far from perfect and they knew it. When they backslid, they slid just as hard as anyone else. Peter gets bashed a lot for having denied Jesus, but Mark 13:50 says, "Then they *all* forsook Him and left Him." The difference in a follower and a disciple is that a disciple keeps coming back, covered in sin and begging forgiveness. There is no other place for the disciple. That doesn't mean that the disciple will never face temptation, relapse, imprisonment, or any other sin that trapped that person. It means that despite everything, that person is commited to Jesus, to carrying out His Kingdom agenda. That person hangs on *every Word* that proceeds from the mouth of God. A disciple knows he will be forgiven, because he already has been and he knows the One who forgives personally and intimately. When you are completely sold out to Jesus, your life becomes His, to do with it as He wills. Don't you know the devil is going to try to throw every temptation he can at the person, to make them doubt, to make them fear, to make them *forget* who they're called to be and what they're called to do? It's the devil's job to get a disciple off their game. You've got to remember who you are, Whose you are, and what you're called to do. You've got to have tenacity, the hard-headed "by any means necessary" mindset to keep getting back up getting back in the game.

I AM SET FREE BY THE TRUTH

*"And you shall know the truth, and **the truth shall make you free.**"*
John 8:32

There's a lot that could be said here, but I want to tell you how this Scripture was fulfilled in my life. When I was first born again, there was another woman in jail that only got visits from a lady that came to minister to her. One day the lady brought some papers that had the woman's name inserted into Biblical confessions on identity in Christ, followed by where that Scripture could be found in the Bible. I was fascinated by that. I wanted a copy of that *so bad* but I didn't know how to get one. When I got out, months later, that list was still on my heart, so I started looking up "identity in Christ" on the computer. I made my own list, which over time grew into several pages. I read those confessions out loud every morning when I had my time with God. I don't remember when exactly, but one day it occurred to me that God's Word is *Truth*, so anything that doesn't agree with it is a *lie*, and *everything, everything, everything* that I had been told, been shown, read, or even thought myself, was a *lie*! I knew that the Bible said that Satan is the father of lies, so I knew that everything I thought about myself or was told I was or had ever been compared to was from the devil. I got *angry!* I realized that *most people*, even Christians, were living the same lie. There were things people said about me, and things that I knew, were facts, but that does not make them Truth. The Bible says that God calls those things which be not as though they are. (Rom. 4:17) God spoke the world into existence when it was without form. (Gen. 1) Day after day, I spoke God's Word over who *He says* I am, believing that He who created me knew who I was more than anybody. I got stronger and stronger. The things people said about me didn't matter anymore. The images the media bombards us with didn't have me comparing myself and falling miserably short. Best of all, my mind was free of negative thinking about myself. I wasn't anything I had ever done. I was who God created me to be. Period. That same freedom is my prayer for *you*, to know the Truth and be set free.

I HEAR JESUS' VOICE AND I FOLLOW HIM

*"My sheep **hear My voice**, and I know them, **and they follow Me.**"*
John 10:27

There are 3 voices in your head- God's, the devil's, and yours. You have to learn to tell the difference. God's voice will never go against His Word. It will never lead you to do anything bad for you. It will often give you a tight feeling in your gut. When God repeats something, to me, He repeats it Word for Word. The devil's voice is accusing. It comes in the form of doubt, discouragement, condemnation, negativity, illusion. The devil speaks twisted truth. When Jesus was in the desert and the devil came to tempt Him, the devil used Scripture in a twisted way, trying to trick Jesus. Jesus spoke the Truth of Scripture right back to him and defeated him. The devil twisted God's Words when he tempted Eve in the Garden of Eden. The devil speaks to a person in their own voice, making them think that it's their own thought. The most extreme usage of this is how the devil speaks to someone to try to get them to take their own life. I know. I've been there many times. Learning to discern Jesus' voice comes from spending time with Him in His Word. If you know His love for you, you will recognize anything that doesn't line up with it. Let's say that you get a letter from someone claiming to be your mom, and they talk about your red hair, and your hair has never been red. They talk about when you were a kid, how you took vacations to the mountains every year, but you only remember going to the beach. The letter is signed in your mom's name, but the handwriting isn't hers and neither is the return address. You would automatically know that it was not from your mother. Jesus loves you and only means good for you. He doesn't berate you or put you down, ever. He's more forgiving than anybody you have ever known. The thing is, you have to recognize when the voice in your thoughts are *not* His, and *immediately* shut it down. Cast it to the feet of Jesus, in Jesus' Name. Speak the Word of God over it. You have authority, in the Name of Jesus. Now, how do you deal with your own voice? By renewing your mind with the Word of God, (Rom. 12:2) so that even your own thoughts are His. And then follow Him. He will take you places you never dreamed of.

I AM ETERNALLY SECURE IN CHRIST

*"And **I give them eternal life, and they shall never perish; neither shall anyone snatch them out of My hand.**" John 10:28*

There is no way possible to "lose" your salvation, even if you stop going to church, even if you continue to sin. It can't be done. How am I so sure? The Holy Spirit is your guarantee. Ephesians 1:13-14 says, "In Him you also trusted, after you heard the Word of Truth, the Gospel of *your salvation*; in Whom also, having believed, *you were sealed with the Holy Spirit of promise, Who is the guarantee of our inheritance* until the redemption of the purchased possession, to the praise of His glory." I have experienced the Holy Spirit in many ways, and I have had many experiences that I know are only possible by the help or gifting of the Spirit. The Spirit of God is undeniable. It was the Holy Spirit who revealed God to me in a way that made me *know* that God was real. God chose you as His before he even created the world. In His own timing, He drew you to Him. He revealed Himself. And you were saved. You were rescued from sin and eternal death. God paid a high price for your salvation. He gave His only Son, Jesus, to pay for your sins. The Person and Work of Jesus Christ is all-sufficient and irrevocable. Nothing and no one has the power to overcome Jesus and what He accomplished at the Cross. Just before taking His last breath, Jesus said, "It is finished."

(Jn. 19:30) The Greek word for "finished" in this verse translates to "paid in full". Your salvation isn't based on anything you do, other than receiving Christ by faith. Christ was the *only* perfect, sinless human, therefore His Blood was the only blood that could atone for the sins of mankind. When you refer to being "covered in the Blood", this is what that means. Romans 6:5 (NIV) brings it all back to eternal security. "If we have been united with Him like this in death, we will certainly also be united with Him in His resurrection." God knew that we were in need of a Savior. It was part of His plan to bring you back home, from the very beginning.

I AM A DISCIPLE

*"By this all will know that **you are My disciples**, if you have love for one another." John 13:35*

A disciple is a student of a particular teacher, with the intention of becoming a teacher to others, according to their teacher's specific training. For instance, John the Baptist taught repentance and baptism. Andrew, who later became a disciple of Jesus and introduced his brother Simon Peter to Jesus, was originally a disciple of John the Baptist. The relationship between disciple and teacher wasn't limited to the classroom. The disciple left home and lived in a continual relationship of devoted learning from their teacher. The objective was to become like their teacher in every way. The focus in learning was not only the content being learned, but also its interpretation, and to be so like the teacher himself that it were no different than having the teacher there. The focus was as much on the teacher as the subject of his teaching. In Matthew 28:19-20, Jesus tells His disciples, "Go therefore and make disciples of all nations, baptizing them in the Name of the Father and of the Son and of the Holy Spirit, teaching them to observe all things that I have commanded you; and lo, I am with you always, even to the end of the age. Amen." You are called to be like Jesus, not just know about Him. You are called to *know Him* intimately, personally, intricately.

The thing that sets you apart from disciples of other teachers is that Jesus' message is, first and foremost, *love*. Everything else that Jesus taught was hinged on love, loving God and loving others, first. As a disciple of Christ, you are also to teach others what Jesus taught-how to love. Love doesn't necessarily have to be hugs and roses. The love Jesus teaches is compassion, caring, unconditional love that always looks for ways to make someone else's life better. That kind of love comes in many quiet forms. A friend of mine was at the grocery store and the man behind her paid for her groceries. Not because she couldn't, but just because. That prompted her to do the same for someone else. That same friend is always looking for ways to bless others, friends and strangers alike. One of the biggest ways to show love to someone is simply to listen to them. Meeting people's physical needs with no expectation of receiving anything at all in return is Biblical love. There are a lot of starving people right where you live. It doesn't matter why they're starving. They still need to be filled, with food and with the message of God's love for them. That's what Jesus' disciples do. You love.

I LOVE OTHERS

*"By this all will know that you are My disciples, if **you have love for one another**." John 13:35*

The world has a very distorted understanding of love. To find the true meaning of *anything*, find out what the Bible says about it. 1 Corinthians 13:4-8 says, "Love suffers long and is kind; love does not envy; love does not parade itself, is not puffed up; does not behave rudely; does not seek its own, is not provoked, thinks no evil; does not rejoice in iniquity, but rejoices in the truth; bears all things, believes all things, hopes all things, endures all things. Love never fails." This is how God defines love. His Word is Truth and He never changes. (Jn. 17:17, Num. 23:19) Love is not just a feeling. It's a spirit itself, and a fruit, or result, of the Holy Spirit living inside you. Like any fruit, when the seed of love is implanted by the Holy Spirit, it takes time to grow. It takes cultivating, pruning, watering, and lots of Son-shine. When love matures, it then bears fruit that yields seed for others. Before the work of the Holy Spirit within me, I was not a loving person. I had no patience. I was rude, self-centered. I felt absolutely hopeless, defeated, unloved and unlovable. I tried my best to isolate from the rest of the world. But thank the Lord, the Spirit of Christ pursued me. 1 John 4:19 says, "We love Him because He first loved us." Jesus poured His love out until it overflowed to people around me. It took time. It was painful sometimes. I was used to my own private world where I didn't have to come out of my comfort zone, but one day I felt God saying in my spirit, "An isolated Christian is a useless Christian." That opened my eyes! Soon after that, I finally came out of isolation. I was reading The Living Bible in the car, on the way to the ministry where I would live. God spoke to me very directly, through 2 Timothy:1:7-8,

"For the Holy Spirit, God's gift, does not want you to be afraid of people, but to be wise and strong, *and to love them and enjoy being with them.* If you will stir up this inner power, you will never be afraid to tell others about our Lord." Well! Speak, Lord! I've learned not only to love, but to be loved, and to enjoy people, rather than try to get away from them as fast as possible. Taking my focus off self and focusing on others has transformed me like no other experience ever has. Jesus tells us that the entire commandments can be summed up in 2 commandments- Loving God and loving others as we love ourselves. It all comes down to love.

I AM JESUS' FRIEND

*"**You are My friends** if you do whatever I command you."* John 15:14

These words coming from anyone else could be a set up. After all, love is unconditional. But coming from Jesus, it could only mean one thing, to love. Love when it hurts. Love when it's hard. Love when you don't *feel* love, when you don't know a person, when you don't like a person. Love if it costs your last dime. Love if it goes against everything other people think is the "right" thing to do. Give hope to the hopeless, help to the helpless. Defend the defenseless. Clothe the poor, visit the sick, pray for everyone, and trust God to help you know where to love and who to love and how to love. God's ways are not our ways, and His thoughts are not our thoughts. (Is. 55:8) It will blow your mind, the ways in which God calls you to love, and the people He places in your life to love. There was a man who came to the ministry that served with me in the kitchen. I thought he hated me. I didn't understand. I tried to be friendly to him, but give him his space at the same time. His attitude toward me only intensified. I didn't know what to do, so I decided to pray for him every morning and every night, as well as every time I saw him or thought of him. After a few days, God spoke into my spirit, "He needs love more than anyone else in this ministry right now." That shocked me. So I made myself love him. One day, after things had started getting a little better, I asked him if I could share something with him. I told him what God had revealed to me, and that I had been praying for him. I told him I thought that he had hated me, but that I knew that there were things he was going through that nobody knew about and that I just wanted the opportunity to make things easier for him and love him as much as he was comfortable with. For the first time since I had known him, he looked at me and smiled. His brow wasn't scrunched up. He thanked me and told me that he was trying to deal with things that he thought no one would understand. I didn't press him for details. It wasn't my business. But when he left the ministry, he called to tell me that he would see me again someday. Jesus said in Matthew 25:40, "Assuredly I say to you, inasmuch as you did it to one of the least of these My brethren, you did it to Me." Jesus will always be the perfect friend to you. Sharing His love with others is how you be the perfect friend back to Him.

I AM APPOINTED TO BEAR FRUIT

*"You did not choose Me, but I chose you and **appointed you that you should go and bear fruit**, and that your fruit should remain, that whatever you ask the Father in My Name He may give you." John 15:16*

In the Parable of the Sower, (Mt. 13) Jesus tells a story about a man sowing seed in different types of soil. The seed represents the Word of God. The only soil that was able to bear fruit was the good soil. The soil couldn't bear the fruit on its own, unless someone came and sowed the seed in it. You are the soil. Someone sowed the seed into you. As the seed grows, you mature and bear fruit. Galatians 5:22-23 tells the fruit of the Spirit, the evidence of the Holy Spirit living and working inside you. "But the fruit of the Spirit is love, joy, peace, longsuffering, kindness, goodness, faithfulness, gentleness, self-control." In the same way that new trees are grown from the seed of another tree's fruit, so does your fruit plant new trees, which will produce its own fruit for other trees to be grown. The Word of God is to be shared by the use of the fruit of the Spirit. Some people can be too aggressive or judgmental when trying to tell someone about Jesus. That scares people away. A really good way to share Jesus is just to be an example of the love He's shown you. Kindness and compassion, to a person who lives a hard, inhumane existence, speaks to the soul. There's a beautiful quote by Maya Angelou, "I've learned that people will forget what you said, people will forget what you did, but people will never forget how you made them feel." I've been one of those people that felt subhuman. Maybe you have, too. As hard-hearted as I had to condition myself to be, I've had complete strangers share small, random acts of kindness that brought me to choking, sobbing, gremlin-faced crying. I couldn't understand why anyone would be motivated to do such things. I know now, it was the love of God, loving me through His people. One of my favorite Scriptures is Acts 10:38, where it says that Jesus "went about doing good". In my mind, I can picture Jesus skipping from person to person with a huge smile on His face, doing all kinds of good stuff for people. Man, I want to be like that! I cleaned bathrooms for a couple of older women for a while, and they would give me all kinds of praise, but I had to tell them that I was the one who was blessed by it, because for the first time in my life, I was able to *give* a blessing, rather than always be the one who needed help. In fact, I felt so blessed by that, I actually felt a little guilty. It felt *that good* to me! In the beginning, you were the soil. As you mature and grow, you become the fruit and your fruit produces seed. Your fruit remains through your seed.

I AM KEPT FROM THE EVIL ONE

*"I do not pray that You should take them out of the world, but that You should **keep them from the evil one.**" John 17:15*

Matthew 28:19 is part of The Great Commission. It says, "Go therefore and make disciples of all nations, baptizing them in the Name of the Father, and of the Son, and of the Holy Spirit." This is talking about missions. Not all missionaries are called to go to Africa. The mission field is wide open, and we are *all* called to be missionaries, starting with right where you are. Your home is a mission field. There are people called to be witnesses to gang members, women who work in the sex industry, bikers, people in prison, drug addicts, people who are homeless. A lot of Christians don't want to associate with "those kind of people", but thank God there are people who do. Jesus said in Luke 5:31-32, "Those who are well have no need of a physician, but those who are sick. I have not come to call the righteous, but sinners, to repentance." The devil will try every conceivable way possible to stop you from snatching someone out of his grip. He takes it personal. Jesus knew that, so He prayed that God would keep the workers of Light from evil, but He also sent them out in pairs, so that there would be accountability. A lot of times, people are called to be witnesses to people who are still involved in the lifestyle that the person witnessing used to be in.

Temptation is all around. You can't be a light to the world if you're still trying to be like the world. And don't think that a person can't be tricked by the devil, even after having a strong walk with the Lord. I let him lead me right back into the same thing Jesus saved me from. All of it. And it started with trying to witness to someone, by myself, who was still in that lifestyle. It was a test that I failed. It took 20 years to get back to that close walk with God, and this time I cherish it and guard it vigorously. I am more determined than ever, though, to share what I've been through and what God has done for me, in order to save other people's souls. You carry Jesus with you everywhere you go. He's inside of you. Don't be afraid, just follow His lead. You were *chosen* to do great things for Him.

I AM NOT OF THE WORLD

"They are not of the world, just as I am not of the world." John 17:16

The word "world" in Greek translates as "orderly arrangement". Jesus was referring to the culture and belief system that rejects God and His authority. As Christians, we are called to be a part of society in order to bring Truth to those around us who walk in darkness. By darkness, I don't necessarily mean they are implicitly evil. Darkness simply means that they do not know God. In most cases, those who walk in darkness don't even know they're in darkness. I didn't, although with all the things I've experienced in my life, it doesn't surprise me. Christians are to be an example, a representative of God's Kingdom. Some people get pretty upset by people that don't go along with the crowd. It angers them that a person would choose to honor God, rather than man, because whether they realize it or not, it exposes the darkness in them, the wrong attitudes or motives or actions that they think no one is aware of. Truth exposes people's weaknesses. Someone trying to present themselves as something that they aren't is extremely protective. Many people who identify themselves with status, money, or any other facade will go to extreme lengths to maintain that identity. This is not even to mention those who try to cover their sin. As a child of light, you are a threat.

Mark 4:17 says "*when* tribulation or persecution arises", not *if.* It will. God promises to be with you *during* those times. In Acts 5, Peter and some of the other apostles were jailed for preaching about Jesus. They were beaten and told not to preach about Jesus, and released. In verses 41-42 it says, "So they departed from the presence of the council, *rejoicing that they were counted worthy to suffer shame for His Name.* And daily in the Temple, and in every house, *they did not cease teaching and preaching Jesus as the Christ.*" They chose to honor God, and not man. And they *rejoiced,* after being jailed and beaten, because it was evidence that they were the real deal, true disciples of Jesus Christ. "If the world hates you, you know that it hated Me before it hated you. If you were of the world, the world would love its own. Yet because you are not of the world, but I chose you out of the world, therefore the world hates you." (Jn. 15"18-19)

I AM SANCTIFIED BY THE WORD OF GOD

"Sanctify them by Your truth. Your Word is truth." John 17:17

To be sanctified means that you are set apart for an intended purpose, in this case, a divine mission. You are on assignment for the Kingdom of God. Your assignment requires you to be set apart spiritually, while living among and influencing people in the world that are not believers. The Word of God sanctifies you. It makes you holy and cleanses you. Ephesians 5:26 refers to this by saying, "that He might sanctify and cleanse her by the washing of the water of the Word". Those things about you that can't be scrubbed off in the shower, such as wrong beliefs, attitudes, behaviors, or other strongholds, are cleansed by the washing of the water of the Word, so that you can help others to know Jesus and live the abundant life that comes only through Him. "To open their eyes, in order to turn them from darkness to light, and from the power of Satan to God, that they may receive forgiveness of sins and an inheritance among those who are sanctified by faith in Me." (Acts 26:18) Another Scripture that comes to mind is Romans 12:2, "And do not be conformed to this world, but be transformed by the renewing of your mind." The Word is Spirit and it is life. (Jn. 6:63) I cannot stress this enough- YOU MUST STAY IN THE WORD! You will be cleansed and equipped for your particular mission through the Word and the

Holy Spirit. God will place people in your path, some to help you, others for you to help. Along the way, you will mature and become strong and bold. You will make a difference in the world around you, helping people become their Christ-designed selves. You will walk into your divine calling, fulfilling *God's plans and purposes* for your life. There is no higher achievement than that. Your mission is a radical move of a radical God. It starts in the Word and transforms everything that is connected to you, everyone that you encounter, and the world around you.

I AM GOD'S GIFT TO CHRIST

*"Father, I desire that **they also whom You gave Me** may be with Me where I am, that they may behold My glory which You have given Me; for You loved Me before the foundation of the world." John 17:24*

There is only one way to eternal life, Jesus Christ. (Jn. 6:65) God the Father gave Jesus authority to grant eternal life to certain people whom God gave to Jesus as a gift. (Jn. 17-6-12) Notice that Jesus says, "they also whom You gave Me", which implies that they were already given to Him, and *then* He asks for them to be with Him. John 6:37 says, "All that the Father has given Me *will come to Me*, and the one who comes to Me I will by no means cast out." "Will come", not "has come". You were specifically chosen before you were even born. You and your children, and their children, for a thousand generations. You are a precious gift to Jesus. He desires for you to be with Him eternally. In fact, you *will*, because He said so. *It is written*. "So now Jesus and the ones He makes holy have the same Father. That is why Jesus is not ashamed to call them His brothers and sisters." (Heb. 2:11 NLT) And in Hebrews 2:13 it says, "Here am I and the children whom God has given Me." You are a special child, a child of the King, a friend and family member of Jesus Christ, the Messiah. Walk like it. Talk like it. Love like it. Fight like it. Surely the God of the entire universe does not give cheap gifts. Think about that. Your value is immense, priceless. God gave the Levites as a gift to the people of Israel, to do the work of the tabernacle. (Num. 18:6) Only those called and chosen and born into that order of priests could do the work. God called and chose you to do His work on this earth. You were born for such a time as this. When Jesus unwraps His gift with your name on it, don't you want Him to be like a child on their birthday? Don't you want to see Jesus ecstatic, overjoyed by His gift, laughing and crying and dancing? Jumping and shouting? I do. And I want to be there to see when He opens *all* His gifts. You are a treasured gift to Jesus. Your life is God's gift to you. What you do with your life is your gift to God. I believe in you, in what is to come in you and through you, because I believe in God. I *know* where I came from. If He can do it for me, He can and will most assuredly do it for you, because HE LOVES YOU, and so do I. God bless you.

Made in the USA
Columbia, SC
13 May 2024

35229745R00180